EYES

IN THE MIND

Library of Congress Catalog Card Number: 93-74625

EYES

IN THE MIND

🍂 🍂 🍂 🍂 🍂

A
Century
of
Vision

at
Oak
Hill
School

Christine Palm

Dedication

*To CIB staff ～ thousands of dedicated women and men
who, over the past one hundred years,
have changed the lives of so many.*

ACKNOWLEDGEMENTS

This book, like the one hundred years of CIB, is the work of many, many people. Just as it has been impossible within these pages to list everyone who has contributed to CIB's success, so too is it impossible to name all the graduates, staff (present and former), parents, friends and program participants who gave us their time, their words and their memories to allow us to tell Oak Hill's story. To all who helped, encouraged and served as our inspiration, thank you.

Thanks also to our colleagues at BESB, our twin sister agency, for making their archives available for this research, and to our many generous donors, without whom our work, and this accounting of that work, would not have been possible.

CREDITS

Written by Christine Palm

Design and Composition by Greta D. Sibley

Photography and Copy Photography by Roger Maynard, Applied Photography, Glastonbury, Connecticut

Published by The Connecticut Institute for the Blind/Oak Hill,

Lars Guldager, Executive Director

Managing Editor, Rebecca Earl

Editorial Assistance by Suzanne Heise and Stephen Earl

Printing by T.B. Simonds, Hartford, Connecticut

Prepress by ImageSet Design, Portland, Maine

©1993

An audio tape of this book is available free of charge. Please call The Connecticut Institute for the Blind/Oak Hill at (203) 242-2274.

Contents

To Be Kind  & Good

1893 – 1896

What we teach the little ones: All those things a happy mother teaches her baby and that a normal baby learns with his eyes. Such as: to eat, to play, to walk, to run, to sing, to pray. To make little things of paper. To be clean and happy, kind and good.

Emily Wells Foster.

The children's orchestra.

The first two Nursery children, Antonio Martello and Antonio Martone.

Three hundred years after the death of Christ, a wealthy young Sicilian virgin was persecuted for her faith. Because she bucked society by speaking her mind and giving her possessions to the poor, a judge ordered some soldiers to cut out her eyes and then burn her.

Inexplicably, she became rooted to the spot where she stood; her attackers could not move her. The fire failed to singe her skin, and her eyes miraculously healed.

The legend of Saint Lucy spread and she soon became the Patron Saint of the Blind. On her feast day, the darkest night of the year, people all over the world celebrate a festival of light with candles and songs.

Sixteen centuries after the death of Lucy, the blind in Connecticut were given another (albeit uncanonized) patron saint. Emily Wells Foster, a proper Victorian matron, had much in common with her wild-spirited forebear.

Like Lucy, Foster was an outspoken advocate for the poor and disheartened. She, too, was more strong-willed than her times would allow. And the circumstances of her death, while far from martyrdom, echo some of the ignominy of Saint Lucy's passing; she left no near relatives and was buried in an unmarked grave.

Like the long-ago saint, Emily Wells Foster was born into a well-to-do family and, owing to a strong philanthropic bent, gave much of her wealth to those less fortunate than she. She moved to West Hartford, Connecticut, from her home in Cape Elizabeth, Maine, in 1875 and promptly became an energetic Sunday School teacher at the Morgan Street Chapel and a volunteer at the Morgan Street Mission in Hartford, an almshouse run by the Congregational Church.

In oil portraits, Foster looks every bit the serious Victorian Lady Bountiful — her hair swept up into a severe knot, her mouth set in a straight, flat line. Her eyes have a doleful cast and she rests a gloved hand on a closed parasol. There is however, one rather raffish note to her regal bearing — an elaborate mink stole cascades over her erect shoulders.

In Hartford in the late 1880s, the social tenor was still cloaked in proper Victoriana; it would be ten years before the veil would begin to fall. One reason is that the fire and brimstone of Puritanical religious fervor still smoldered, and fear of Hell, and the tacit connection it had to public outcasts, held a firm grip on the city's mores. Many of society's less fortunate were mistreated; at best, they were misunderstood.

To be sure, some strides had been made locally years earlier for both the deaf and the mentally ill. The American School for the Deaf, the country's first, had been founded in Hartford in 1817. And the Hartford Retreat (now the Institute of Living) became the nation's third hospital when it was founded in 1822 to assist (in the administration's own words) "the distracted, the despondent, the tempted and the broken in heart."

Similar advances for the blind were lacking in Connecticut, however; local society still had a long way to go in doing justice to its citizens with visual impairment, despite the fact that several other states were already forming special schools for the blind. In 1832 in Massachusetts, for example, the well-respected Perkins Institute was founded in Watertown and the more fortunate among Connecticut's blind citizens received schooling there.

Still, even with the establishment of special schools, the fact remained that the blind, as a group, were fairly anonymous. This phenomenon, which was both local and national, had three root causes: patronizing protectiveness on the part of some, indifference on the part of others, and erroneous census figures which vastly underreported the numbers of blind Americans. The first two reasons are fairly easy to imagine — most societies in the world dance between pity and disregard when it comes to those with disabilities.

But the third reason is intriguing because it gives a glimpse into the dynamic of personal and familial response to blindness. The federal government first required census takers to enumerate cases of blind citizens in 1830. For decades thereafter, however, the figures fluctuated wildly: the censuses of 1870 and 1880 had a discrepancy of two hundred percent because census takers, who were paid a bonus of five cents for every blind person they turned up, deliberately doubled the numbers in that ten-year span.

A more disheartening reason for the confusion surfaced by 1920 when the blind were counted at 57,444 nationally. That same year, however, the same reporting source (the U.S. Census Bureau) produced a second figure which was more than 20,000 higher. It seems this discrepancy arose because census workers were so unaccustomed to thinking about blindness that often they simply forgot to inquire about any blind family members. Another (and perhaps more revealing) reason is that many families denied having a blind member, choosing instead to keep their private "shame" a secret. This decision, based in fear, further invalidated the place of blind citizens in society at large.

Although the Connecticut General Assembly required town selectmen to report the number of blind and deaf persons in their towns as early as 1829 (and so took official notice of them), in general, as little light shone in the minds of the sighted as did in the eyes of the blind.

An early description of life for them, reprinted in an early annual report, reads: "The blind were considered…a separate class, hopeless objects of pity, classified with the insane, paupers and such…"

Into this society, on an August afternoon in 1888, Emily Wells Foster stepped out of a teeming Hartford mission house into Morgan Street in search of a child. She had heard from another volunteer that "a blind baby was making a commendable fight for a place in the world, within a stone's throw of the Mission building"[1] in a run-down tenement.

Foster made her way to the tenement and, while groping along the darkened walls, she found the object of her search, literally tripping over the child as he sat motionless and silent on the dank floor.

He was three years old and his name was Antonio Martello. The isolation of his blindness was magnified by his complete lack of facility with English, and in a later account of the day Foster found him, he was described as "feeble, deformed and unpromising…his life was absolutely devoid of interest or occupation."[2] Undaunted, Foster, who was proficient in classical Italian, set about learning vernacular Italian so she could communicate with the child.

She soon found another blind child, an infant whose mother left him in his crib all day out of fear and shame. Foster convinced the distracted young mother to entrust her with the baby. She took the little boy, along with Antonio Martello, to her own home to live with her. Between the years 1888 and 1893, Foster cared for six blind children in this way, calling her loosely

Many of society's less fortunate were mistreated; at best, they were misunderstood.

1. Anonymous author, from an early term paper in the CIB archives.
2. Ibid.

PRESIDENTS OF THE BOARD OF DIRECTORS

Frank E. Cleaveland......................1893–1902
G. Pierrepont Davis......................1902–1907
Rockwell Harmon Potter.............1907–1957
Harvey K. McArthur....................1957–1967
Robert L. Edwards 1967–1977
William H. Thompson 1977–1980
Mary P. Cheney...........................1980–1988
Jerald D. Hassett 1988–1991
Thomas J. Gallagher 1991–1993
John J. Dwyer 1993–

SUPERINTENDENTS

Emily Wells Foster 1893–1902
George H. Marshall 1902–1918
Gordon Hicks 1918–1946
Frank Johns, Jr. 1946–1976
Lars Guldager..............................1977–

organized efforts the "Heart-Sunshine Society."

In her quiet, dignified, but very deliberate manner, Emily Wells Foster had formed what is considered the nation's first nursery for blind children in a clapboard bungalow at 57 Kenyon Street in Hartford's West End neighborhood. It had a large center chimney, a wide front porch with an overhanging eave, and two enormous maples shading the sunny front yard.

In time, it would become known as the Connecticut Institution and Industrial Home for the Blind, then the Connecticut Institute for the Blind and, eventually, CIB/Oak Hill School. It is best known today, however, simply as Oak Hill. Despite several name changes over the years, the institution that grew from Foster's efforts would change forever the lives of hundreds of blind Americans and their families.

If Foster was the blind community's patron saint, Frank E. Cleaveland was its guardian angel.

Cleaveland, a Hartford attorney who became blind three months after being admitted to the Connecticut bar, was Foster's right-hand man in the establishment of her home and, eventually, her school.

Bringing his considerable legal acumen to bear on the state legislature at the time, Cleaveland lobbied hard for Foster's cause. In this way, Cleaveland was instrumental in creating a statewide system of services to the blind, which essentially had two branches — public and private. In 1893, he filed the Articles of Association of the Connecticut Institution and Industrial Home for the Blind, which became the private arm of the system. That same year saw the establishment of the State Board of Education of the Blind — the first such commission for the blind in the nation — which became the public arm. Known today as Board of Education and Services for the Blind (BESB), the organization was founded with Cleaveland as its first secretary, Foster as assistant secretary and Mr. George Marshall, a graduate of the Perkins Institute, as treasurer.

Soon after, Cleaveland appointed an advisory board that included among its thirteen members some of the most distinguished Hartford family names — Stearns, Goodrich, Burr, Pope, Olmstead and Goodwin.

Knowing well the importance of earning one's own livelihood despite a physical barrier, Cleaveland's personal concern was the employment of the blind in suitable, dignified work. Because of this passion, in 1894 he helped Foster establish a Trades Department for blind adults at 334 Wethersfield Avenue in Hartford at a cost of fourteen thousand dollars.

By now the late 19th Century world was lurching toward a new era. It was just a few years before the Spanish-American War. Soon, Wilhelm Konrad Roentgen would discover X-rays, Guglielmo Marconi would invent the wireless and Marie and Pierre Curie would discover radium.

Social progress, too, was being made. In Connecticut, women were granted permission to vote for school officials, and the legislature outlawed factory work for children under fourteen years of age.

Hartford in the late 1890s was exploding into the Machine Age with pneumatic tires, automatic pistols, electric cars and the patents — and insurance — to cover them.

In the city, a heady swell of Yankee ingenuity supplanted the general economic depression of the 1870s and 1880s. Colt Firearms, the Pope Manufacturing Works, Weed Sewing Machine, Royal Typewriter, Billings & Spencer, and Veeder-Root were all staking out their technological turf, with much of the commercial activity centered in the city's Frog Hollow neighborhood. This burgeoning industry gave birth to a new middle class whose fortunes were riding on the wheels, belts and pulleys of manufacturing. While factories sprang up in the north end, too, most of the Northeast and Blue Hills neighborhoods were still rural and dominated by farms.

The settlement of the Upper Albany and Asylum Hill sections of town as fashionable residential areas soon followed. And with the extension of trolley lines and the opening of Keney Park's 663 acres in 1896 (making it one of the largest parks in New England), the Northeast and Northwest neighborhoods began to draw more fashionable families. Factory foremen were building grand homes near those of their machinists and brickmakers and the earlier dairy farming families.

Meanwhile, in her sunny nursery on Kenyon Street, Emily Wells Foster continued to lead her quieter revolution. In her understated way, Foster described her early efforts in an annual report, allowing only a trace of self-satisfaction to seep through: "This branch of our work, of taking children before school age, even in their babyhood, is unique as far as I have been able to ascertain. It has not been undertaken by any other institution for the blind in the world."

Within one year of its operation, Foster's Kenyon Street nursery was bursting at the seams. In 1894, with Cleaveland's help in securing both General Assembly approval and funding of twenty-eight thousand dollars, Foster bought and equipped a building at 1205-1207 Asylum Avenue in Hartford as a true nursery. By Thanksgiving of 1894, fifteen teachers, aides and matrons taught, comforted, bathed, fed and played with the twenty children who called it their home.

One of these matrons was Lillian Russell. Russell

soon became a pillar of the institution whose contributions of time, talent and compassion would last until her death in 1957 at the age of eighty-four.

Gert DeLeo, an alumna who lived at the Nursery from the time she was nine months old until she was fifteen years of age, was with Russell when she died. DeLeo recalled:

"Lillian Russell was a remarkable woman with a double gift; she had an old-fashioned understanding of children's need to be protected and a progressive understanding of their need to be challenged. Because her time with the school began so very long ago, people tend to overlook how forward-thinking she was."

But before progressive thought could even by entertained by the women caring for these blind children, basic health needs had to be addressed. For this reason, Foster's nursery was, by all accounts, more like a nursing facility. The children ranged in age from three to thirteen and all had been so badly neglected that their health and happiness, rather than their education, were the primary concerns.

...before a child can pick up the violin, he must first pick up his spirits...

The validity of Foster's focus on physical and emotional well-being was borne out decades later by Stetson K. Ryan, executive secretary of BESB, who postulated that neither the gift of sight nor supreme intelligence accounted for success in life. In 1933, at the celebration of the fortieth anniversaries of both the Connecticut Institute for the Blind and BESB, Ryan said: "What, you ask, has been accomplished in these forty years? Have blind people found more complete acceptance by a questioning public because of the service rendered? Have they found opportunity for more abundant living? Are they better citizens for the benefactions of private philanthropy and the state?"

To answer these questions, Ryan cited a study of 610 blind or nearly blind persons who had received "academic or commercial instruction, or trades training" by the Connecticut Institute for the Blind with the support of BESB. Approximately half of these people, the study showed, were self-supporting and successful by the standards of the day.

"As 49 percent of them were totally blind and the remaining 51 [percent] had severe visual impairment, the element of sight, it would seem, is just about a toss-up," concluded Ryan. "Was it because some of the them had vision at one time in their lives [and] knew what the world is like from visual experience? No, that does not seem to be a predominating factor [as] 44 percent were blind at birth or under one year of age; only 19 percent lost their sight at age sixteen or over.

> *Lillian Russell had an old-fashioned understanding of children's need to be protected and a progressive understanding of their need to be challenged.*

Was it because of superior mental ability? The answer to that is that only two of the group were above the average in mental ability; 92 percent, however, were rated as average; nearly 6 percent were given a mental rating below average and one was rated as feebleminded."

What accounted, then, for their success in life? It was, he said, simply this: "good health and an ability to live and work amicably with their fellows."

Four decades earlier, with no formal training in the care or education of the blind, Emily Wells Foster had reached the same conclusion. Under her care, blind children, like "little French Pierre from Meriden," began to thrive for the first time in their lives.

An article printed in *Connecticut Magazine* in 1899 describes the life of this boy, who was not atypical of Foster's charges.

"At seven years of age, the muscles from disease had become weak and useless. In fact the little fellow's life had been chiefly spent in bed. The pale, unintelligent child was taken in charge immediately...and in three months he could walk about the house and enter heartily into kindergarten games. No wonder when he waked in the night he used to sing 'Ring, ring happy bells!'"[3]

Once such children were given the medical and emotional attention they craved, they were ready and eager to concentrate on academic areas of instruction, which Foster described as: "reading by 'line tape,' reading and writing by the Braille method, writing in 'square hand,' (this being done with a grooved board and pencil), number work by means of a type slate, language, history, and zoology."

Foster's maternal leanings are evident in an aside she makes concerning this last discipline: "This last study is one of the most interesting, it being so satisfactorily comprehended by means of stuffed or clay models. Anything that comes within a touch of a blind child it feels it 'can see.'"

---

3. Stone, Rev. George M. From "Work for the Blind in Connecticut" *Connecticut Magazine*, 1899

Music, as well as knitting and Sloyd[4] carpentry, played a vital part in the children's development, as well. "Music," Foster writes, "is a prime factor in the education of the blind. We do not teach it merely as an accomplishment; it means far more than that; it trains, develops, it refines, and as a source of livelihood for many of those deprived of sight, it has been the most available of all pursuits... While we do not claim that all blind people are musical, naturally, living in a world of sound, as our people do, the sense of hearing is highly cultivated and becomes acute..."[5]

But before a child can pick up the violin, he must first pick up his spirits, and Foster knew this instinctively. In a small brown folder printed in 1896, she describes her simple, critical work:

"What We Teach the Little Ones: All those things a happy mother teaches her baby and that a normal baby learns with his eyes. Such as: To eat, to walk, to play, to run, to sing, to pray. To make little things of paper. To be clean and happy, to be kind and good."

---

4. According to Kenneth Stuckey, research librarian at the Perkins Institute, "Sloyd," the Swedish word for woodworking, was a system of teaching the carpenter's craft that emphasized accuracy, measuring and fine planing through the creation of detailed joints.

5. Foster, Emily Wells. From an early report to the Board of Directors.

CHAPTER TWO

Years of Struggle

1897–1900

… The blind have far more in common than not with the rest of society; …it comes down to this: for the blind, the world's image is stamped not on the cornea, but on the heart and the mind, where it is for all of us indelible.

Early Nursery students.

Turn-of-the-century music students. Note Braille music on their laps.

As the turn of the century drew near, the Connecticut Institute for the Blind, with its Nursery-Kindergarten Department and its Trades Department, found itself with more and more students and fewer and fewer financial resources. Pressured by increased demand for its services and dwindling state appropriations, Cleaveland, Foster and Marshall found themselves at a crossroads. By September of 1898, the Trades Department, with thirty-one blind adults in its care, had exactly $89.10 in its coffers.

Meanwhile, the Nursery-Kindergarten Department, with twenty-seven children, had already outgrown its building on Asylum Avenue, and prospects for a new building looked dim.

In its fourth annual report, sent in 1897 to Connecticut Governor Lorrin A. Cooke, the Institute's advisory board did not mince words in expressing its chagrin at how dramatically the State's earlier support had waned, and the board openly criticized the government for its unwillingness to give the money it had promised earlier:

"The failure of the Legislature to provide an adequate appropriation needed by this Department, and the consequent struggle it has undergone to maintain an existence" compelled the institution's leaders to appeal directly to "all public spirited and benevolent people of Connecticut, who believe that our State should not fail to keep abreast with other states and countries, in the discharge of its duty to its citizens…"

In an eloquent testimony later in the annual report, Frank Cleaveland pleads CIB's case by comparing the urgency of the blind's educational needs to a recent, devastating fire that clearly loomed large in everyone's memory at the time. Thus, by skillfully blending rhetoric with fact, Cleaveland drove

A human pyramid.

home the state's responsibility to live up to its promise:

"…the people of Hartford were shocked and thrown into a great state of excitement by the sudden collapse in the night of one of the principal hotels…all knew that beneath the debris of timbers and brick there were many persons undoubtedly yet alive…and in imminent danger of perishing amid the flames.

"The city was stirred to its center. The people with but a single impulse thronged the streets. The militia was summoned and the Fire and Police Departments, with unparalleled energy, began the work of rescue, nor did their activity abate until every brick and timber that might hold down and imperil the life of a human being had been cleared away. And as one after another of the buried victims of the disaster were lifted out of their perilous position, there went up from the assembled thousands a glad and triumphant shout.

"Let us suppose that at this time some would-be guardian of the City Treasury had undertaken to hinder the work of rescue by raising the question of expense, by pointing out that there was a depleted treasury, and that the city could not afford to expend money for this purpose. How would such a proposition have been received by its citizens?"

Cleaveland went on to point out that since there was at the time roughly one blind person for every thousand sighted ones, the cases of "hardship" multiplied throughout the state's citizenry, and so the

Institution's work was critical to all of society.

Cleaveland's summation of the condition of the blind in society in 1898 was paraphrased in a magazine article of the day. Although nearly one hundred years old, parts of his theories are remarkably true to the tenets of CIB today. Then, as now, there are certain things we all — sighted or blind — must understand.

"Mr. Cleaveland has stoutly and persistently claimed from the beginning; first, that blindness itself is not an impassable barrier preventing a person with this limitation from becoming a self-reliant, self-sustaining and useful member of society. Second, that the only reason why all blind people who are otherwise mentally and physically sound, do not become self-sustaining is not because they are blind but because the general belief entertained by all their seeing friends (including their parents) has, in the case of children, robbed them of that training and discipline essential to a successful career…and, in the case of the adult blind, operating to confirm them in the belief that they are rendered helpless by the loss of sight. Third, that Connecticut, in its labors for the blind, (to say nothing of what our sister states have done) is twenty years behind even our neighbors in South America."[1] (It must be pointed out here that through these early efforts of the Connecticut Institute for the Blind,

> …blindness itself is not an impassable barrier preventing a person with this limitation from becoming a self-reliant, self-sustaining and useful member of society…

---

1. Stone, Rev. George M., *Connecticut Magazine.*

21

Early Braille writers.

Connecticut's care of the blind soon surpassed that of other states.)

As the century came to a close, Cleaveland and Foster had been pleading their case for five years, and their written testimony begins to sound tinged with weariness: "The most discouraging and difficult feature of the problem (of blindness)" was not the blindness itself, but rather being forced to "discover or foresee how many times we shall be obliged to make out a case, and before how many different General Assemblies of the State we shall be summoned to appear and be required to meet and overcome the same prejudices, or, more correctly, prejudgment of persons wholly unacquainted with the achievements of the blind."[2]

Among these achievements, which were deemed outstanding personal feats at the same time they were considered typical occupations for the blind, were bookbinding, farming, mining, piano tuning, stenography, crystal cut-

---

2. Cleaveland, Frank, and Foster, Emily Wells. In a report to the Board of Directors explaining their frustration with legislative inaction.

ting, weaving, basketry, and clock and watchmaking and repair.

But it was for the deeper achievements of the blind that both Cleaveland and Foster, along with their ally George Marshall, cared most. Early journals and reports indicate that Cleaveland felt Foster and Marshall were alone among sighted people in understanding the blind.

Like him, they knew the blind have far more in common than not with the rest of society; that it comes down to this: for the blind, the world's image is stamped not on the cornea, but on the heart and the mind, where it is for all of us indelible.

GERT DELEO

I'm glad I had the experience of learning how to be blind without sighted interference. We had to learn to be self-sufficient and the teachers at Oak Hill didn't pander to us. We did everything ourselves, and I would never give that up. I think it's a shame Braille isn't used much anymore. I don't see those years as overly protective at all, even though we were all together, as a family, on the campus.

I remember how much fun we had. We'd have picnics in Elizabeth Park and go somersaulting on the grass. One time, we all came back from summer vacation and we celebrated being back together by sneaking food into our rooms and throwing ourselves a little party. Well, we got pretty rowdy and threw grape juice all over the place. It got on the ceiling, so I got up on a dresser to wash it off. The other kids were handing me up the wet sponges. Then the teacher came in and discovered we were washing off all the calcimine!

I guess the trend toward mainstreaming and teaching the blind in the home is good, but I still wouldn't give up my Oak Hill years for anything. I believe there should be a time and a place where blind kids can get together and share common problems and help each other. You know, share insight.

I have loved my time at Oak Hill and my life afterward. I've been luckier than any of my siblings and luckier than most people I know. I have had a wonderful career as a music teacher (at the Mansfield Training School), I have a home I love and I have had wonderful friends.

Life isn't all right all the time; we just did the best we could. I didn't have my sight, but I have had so much more…

Gert DeLeo died on November 12, 1993, just a few weeks after she said these words. Throughout her life, and her long illness, her unflagging spirit and love of Oak Hill were an inspiration to all who knew her.

Death, Rebirth & 'Worldly Curiosity'

1901 – 1919

They can't see it, but they'll know it's there!

The first graduating class.

An evening's recreation in the parlor.

A sledding expedition, circa 1910.

Chair caning in the Trades Department.

New Nursery in Farmington, Connecticut.

Students tend the cows.

In the first few years of the new century, both the school and Nursery of the Connecticut Institute for the Blind had again outgrown their quarters, including the new building on High Street in Farmington into which the Nursery had moved in 1905. Word of the Nursery and school had spread and increasing numbers of fearful, hopeful parents turned their attention to the remarkable progress being made at the school.

In 1902, Emily Foster, sensing that she was slowing down and that it was time to hand the reins to someone else, asked Superintendent George Marshall to assume direct responsibility for overseeing the school. In his annual report for the years 1903 to 1904, Marshall wrote convincingly of the need for more space. Although Marshall's exhortation paints a bleak picture of the institution's facilities, it gives a vivid account of how lively and thriving the school had become.

"Our main building was formerly a dwelling house arranged for two families, which in the beginning of the work, when it was in the nursery stage, answered the purpose very well, but since we have grown into a fairly large school it is in no sense of the word suited to our needs. The school rooms are small and ill-ventilated, and the dormitories are very much crowded. Owing to the fact that we have no playrooms, we are obliged to let the children use their sleeping rooms during the day more than is desirable, but there is no alternative.

"Then the kinds of work [we do] are dissimilar and interfere very much; this is especially so in the case of our literary and music departments. We have about thirty children in the music department, some of

Foster was endowed naturally with infinite tenderness and sympathy…

whom study piano, violin and a wind instrument, and must in consequence have time to practice upon each. This means that about every available room in the house, including dining and sleeping rooms is occupied, almost every hour in the day, by aspiring young musicians. In order that our children develop well, both mentally and morally, it is very essential that they should have good physical training; this is given them as far as is possible, but we feel the need of much larger play grounds than they have now, where the children may feel perfectly free and independent."

These words, which sound dated and quaint to the modern ear, must be looked at in the context of the era in which they were written. "Freedom" and "independence" — especially for children — were not sanctioned by most of adult society. The Victorian world had yet to shake off the dour Puritan world view that the only way to get close to God was to suffer. And so children, like everyone else, were expected to subjugate their happiness for less worldly pursuits.

From the start, however, those associated with the school's mission fought fiercely for the rights of children. Foster, Cleaveland, Marshall, Russell and the other early proponents were unwilling to wait for society to catch up with them. Their enlightened view that children have inherent rights as citizens was often at odds with society's view that children should be seen and not heard, and that blind children should be neither seen *nor* heard.

These early leaders also valued the child's right to be happy. They did not believe that blindness robbed children of their natural tendency toward joy and spontaneity. In fact, it often seems that the pupils were considered not blind children, but children who happened to be blind, and they expected the students to feel all the same emotions of sighted children. It is this attitude which has kept the school forward-thinking throughout its history.

In 1907, the Connecticut Institute for the Blind's Board of Directors elected as its president the Rev. Rockwell Harmon Potter, pastor of Center Congregational Church. Potter, who later became the Dean of Hartford Seminary, was a man known for his booming oratory, tenacity for furthering enlightened causes, and unconventional teaching style. He was known to take more than one first-year seminarian into an empty church, march the unsuspecting student to the pulpit and then bellow from the nave, "You have twenty minutes to save my soul!"

With dedication that soon became legendary, Potter served the Institution for an astonishing fifty years, until his retirement in 1957 — just eighteen months before his death.

In 1910, the school received both a terrible blow and a great boost. Frank Cleaveland, who had laid such a firm foundation for the fledgling school, died in Washington, D.C., where he had been named principal of the Columbia Polytechnic Institute for the Blind. His death at age fifty-two was a shock to his Connecticut friends who owed so much to his efforts just sixteen years earlier.

That same year, however, the school came of age as an institution when it received its first major donation from a private individual. The gift allowed the struggling Institute to create in Farmington a new nursery for its blind children by rehabilitating an old home there known as the Wollenberg Homestead. This generous gift, coming as it did from a member of the general public, proved that care of the blind was not only a duty to be undertaken by educators and state agencies, but was, in fact, worthy of private philanthropic largesse. The tale of this gift is a remarkable one and indicates how changeable were the fortunes of the institution in its early years.

M.J. Morrissey, a doctor from Unionville, was one of a growing number of professionals who volunteered their services to the school and nursery. One night, Dr. Morrissey made an emergency call to attend the young son of Mrs. H. R. Cromwell of Philadelphia, who was staying at the Elm Tree Inn in Farmington. Mrs. Cromwell was a widow visiting her daughter, a student at Miss Porter's School. (Mrs. Cromwell's late husband's name was, oddly, Commodore Oliver Cromwell.)

Apparently, Mrs. Cromwell felt so indebted to the good doctor that she offered to help one of his favorite causes. In jest, Morrissey suggested a new nursery for the overcrowded one he was about to visit. Within a month, Mrs. Cromwell had convinced a wealthy suitor, Mr. E.T.

Rockwell Harmon Potter.

Stotesbury (one of the partners in the firm of J. Pierpont Morgan, Inc.) to provide the funds.

In a lighthearted passage from his 1914 "Dedicatory Address," Rockwell Harmon Potter relates the incident (perhaps with apocryphal overtones): "Mr. Stotesbury, in the excess of his delight and joy at the success of his quest [to woo Mrs. Cromwell], offered anything

31

OF BENEVOLENCE &
A BUSHEL OF ORANGES

November 5, 1952

Mr. Daniel Campion
111 Pearl Street
Hartford, Connecticut

Dear Dan:

After the meeting of the Directors of the Blind Institute last week, you asked me to record the narrative of the benevolent gift of Mr. E.T. Stotesbury of Philadelphia which expedited the growth of the modest little home for the blind in Farmington.

At that time it housed twelve children. Miss Russell was the superintendent. I was their doctor while practicing in Unionville and Farmington. A few weeks before Christmas, about forty-five years ago, I had occasion to make a medical call on Mrs. Commodore Oliver Cromwell of Philadelphia at the Elm Tree Inn in Farmington. Her son Jimmie, who later became Minister to Canada, had received an ugly cut over the eye while skating, and I also took care of that. When I had finished she asked me where my next call might be. I told her that I was calling on twelve blind children in a very inadequate little home on High Street in Farmington, and that it was my pet charity in thanksgiving that my own children were blessed that she might name as a betrothal present: a dog-collar of pearls or a tiara of diamonds — or anything of that sort. Her reply was, as reported, that she had a bureau of such trash and didn't need any more or want any more to bother with. I was not present and cannot give direct evidence of the phrases she used. I know this, however. She did say, 'I have found here in Farmington a little cottage on the High Street, as I walked the lovely ways of Farmington, where two devoted women are caring for blind babies in utterly inadequate facilities. If you want to do something to please me, provide this Connecticut Institute for the Blind with the means to get an adequate house for that nursery for blind

with normal eyes. I remarked that she too should be grateful to God that her daughter of about ten years was blessed with beauty and normal eyesight. Mrs. Cromwell then said, "When you make your call at the Institute please return to the Inn and let me know if there is something I can do for them at Christmas."

I did so, and felt sure she had in mind a bushel of oranges. Mrs. Cromwell asked me, "What have you thought of?" I replied, "It would be wonderful if you could build them a new home." She answered, "Mr. E.T. Stotesbury of Philadelphia is going to call on me tomorrow. Will you have lunch with us at the Farmington Club?"

While at lunch I reviewed the story of the children, and told Mr. Stotesbury I thought fifteen thousand dollars would do for a starter for the home. He said, "Do you know of a place we can get in Farmington?" I said, "I know of a place which one of the Farmington ladies has offered me for six thousand dollars, if I would move from Unionville to Farmington."

Mr. Stotesbury said, "Let's get into the old barouche and look at the place." He asked me to go in to talk with the owner. I offered her five thousand dollars cash, and she agreed. The transaction took less than five minutes, because I did not wish to keep the Big Wheel waiting. When I returned to the barouche he inquired, "Wasn't she at home?" I said, "Yes, I bought the place for five thousand dollars." Mrs. Cromwell said, "You shouldn't have bargained with her. Didn't you tell me she was a widow?" I said, "Yes, but it isn't my money, it's Mr. Stotesbury's." Mr. Stotesbury said to Mrs. Cromwell, "Let him alone. If he weren't practicing medicine I'd take him with me to Philadelphia, when he can pull off a fifteen thousand dollar proposition like that in an hour."

My friend, the late R.F. Jones, remodelled the house with fourteen rooms for thirteen thousand five hundred dollars. Mrs. Morrissey and I spent two whole days at Neal, Goff and Ingalls and bought all of the furnishings for fifteen hundred dollars.

When we had the dedication, the first names to sign in the book were Anna Roosevelt Cowles, wife of Admiral Cowles and sister of Teddy, Theodore Pope and Michael J. You asked for it, so there it is.

Incidentally, I have had three other productive solicitations which I might relate to you in person at another time. One was the whole summer's milk supply from the Porter School herd to St. Agnes' Home for over twenty years — estimated to be worth about twenty-eight thousand dollars. A gift to St. Francis Hospital of eighty-five hundred dollars from Miss Grace Bliss of Scarborough Street, Hartford. A gift of one thousand dollars to St. Patrick's Church in Farmington from Theodore Pope.

While Aetna has done all right, Dan, I'm telling you they missed out on a good salesman. I do very well with other people's money, but I still have a mortgage on my house.

Sincerely,

Michael J. [Morrissey]

babies. They have tried to get it from these Connecticut Yankees, but you know how tight they are!'"

And thus, the story goes, the weary doctor Morrissey's jest yielded a large new nursery on Garden Street in Farmington. In a letter to Mr. Daniel Campion (a board member at the time), Morrissey confessed that he had expected, as a donation from Mrs. Cromwell, "perhaps a bushel of oranges."

Within a year, the school department, too, was on the move.

In 1911, Marshall saw his dream for more space realized when the school department moved to an impressive new location on Holcomb Street in Hartford, (where it remains to the present day). Reconfirming its early support of the institution, the state legislature appropriated fifty-thousand dollars for the new building.

The land was guarded by several massive oak trees, which provided both shade and a patrician air. They soon became part of the school's identity, but it wasn't until the 1950s that the Connecticut Institution for the Blind added Oak Hill School to its name.

Nineteen girls and twenty-five boys took the first steps to their independence as they strolled out over twenty shaded acres of land. Much was made of the new site, including some criticism that the splendid land was wasted on children who could not see it.

To this judgment the indefatigable Potter is reputed to have hollered, "They can't see it, but they'll know it's there!"

As indeed they did. Long before the rest of society caught up with them, Marshall and his colleagues recognized a child's innate empathy with the natural world, and so farming, gardening and tending animals became an integral part of life at Oak Hill in its early decades.

Boys play with a pet rabbit on the Oak Hill farm.

Marshall wrote movingly — and extensively — of life "on the hill" and his words are testimony to the special new world the school's blind children and their teachers were creating together. The days were long, and full, and much was expected of the students, who seemed to welcome the labor because they shared in its fruits. On the sprawling campus, the administration's tact was strict but empathetic; offering both challenge and support, responsibility and freedom. And although deprived of the sense of sight, there is no question that the children enjoyed days filled with sensuousness and light.

"The ample grounds of the school are an ever increasing source of pleasure and improvement to the pupils," Marshall said. "A good beginning was made in the garden in 1911…A large pine, with a trunk over two feet in diameter, and several old apple trees were cut down, and the boys sawed them into four-foot lengths, then split these into kindling…We are still using the wood which they prepared and there is enough left for our winter supply.

"The following spring work began in earnest. The fruit trees of which we have a number were sprayed with lime and sulphur… Under careful supervision the larger boys set out a number of young fruit and grape vines. They removed the earth carefully, keeping the upper and the subsoil separate; planted the trees and replaced the earth, being sure to put the fine soil around the roots and packing it down well at the bottom of the hole, and then putting the subsoil on top…After the plowing was done the pupils helped with the harrowing and smoothing up…"[1]

Many years later, in his term paper "Fifty Years and a Bit More: Being a Brief But Comprehensive Survey of the Education of the Blind in Connecticut," Oak Hill alumnus John J. Duffy of Hartford remembers: "…Those chores which could be done by blind children were assigned to them — such as spading the chicken-run; caring for the chickens, weeding the garden, sorting vegetables, and all such healthy chores — oh yes! — that included even milking the cows! We did them, and willingly."

Set against the pastoral life on campus was the outbreak, in 1914, of World War I. Most likely, the students at Oak Hill, like their peers at other schools, were fairly insulated from the reality of the war. It was, nonetheless, to have a profound effect on their adult lives. The horror of the world's first modern war had one bright side: it gave rise to a crucial development in the progress of the blind.

This change grew out of a new and terrifying form of technology — the nerve and mustard gases which blinded thousands of young soldiers. Ironically, it was the Germans who made a discovery that would turn this shame into something good for all nations. The German government had long used German shepherds as police dogs and to sniff out escapees or to find dead bodies in the fields. But now, like the Allies, they had a new "army" of young blind men to contend with, and so they began to train these shepherds as companions to blind soldiers.

In 1929, a Swiss woman named Dorothy Harrison Eustis used this wartime discovery to establish "The Seeing Eye," the first guide dog school, in Morristown, New Jersey. Almost immediately, "seeing eye" dogs were trained for peacetime use by scores of adult blind citizens, offering a kind of freedom and self-sufficiency they had never known before. Other programs to train seeing eye dogs followed, including Connecticut's well-known FIDELCO program.

---

1. Marshall, George. From his introductory remarks in the Annual Report of 1911–12, CIB archives.

In 1915, while the war raged, Oak Hill's School Department celebrated the graduation of its first *bona fide* class of pupils. With great pomp and joy, students Ethel Luella Harvey, Angela L. Coffey, Burton R. Beavon, Robert E. Kelly and Emil A. Johnson left the institution well-prepared for their new life outside the school's walls. Only one returned to the protective arms of Oak Hill.

Superintendent Marshall wrote "Of the five who graduated in June, three entered the Perkins Institute for the Blind at Watertown, Massachusetts; another remained at home for a year's rest; and one returned, as it seemed best, for an additional year's work."

At the graduation ceremony, Ethel Harvey, who was class valedictorian, addressed an eager throng of parents, teachers, administration, staff and fellow students. Sadly, no copy of her essay, "The Debt We Owe Our Dreamers" remains. And yet one can't help judge from its title that Harvey, like her fellow students, felt she was leaving a place that was both visionary and practical.

The titles of the other students' essays are equally revealing, offering a glimpse into both the school's life and the tenor of the times: "The Temperance Cause," "The Boy Scout Movement," (scouting had been established in Connecticut in 1907), "The Panama Canal," (the canal had just opened the year before), and "Poultry Raising."

The poultry farm of Oak Hill had a long, productive life span and was, by all accounts, a source of great fascination for the students. In his history paper, John Duffy writes: "After a while the boys thought it would be a good idea to let the girls take over the chicken project. The girls took charge of it until they began to forget to feed the chickens. So the boys decided that (perhaps) that was not such a good idea…"

Gert DeLeo had a different memory of the chicken enterprise. "Some of us joined the 4-H Club and took care of the chickens," DeLeo recalled. "The girls had three coops, with two girls to a coop. We'd clean them and collect the eggs. We didn't like ringing doorbells and having the people say no, so we made a deal with the boys: we'd collect and clean their eggs if they'd sell ours. It was all very good experience — in cooperation and in responsibility. And it gave us a nice place to go when it was cold." Years later, when the poultry operation was no longer feasible, the school's Board of Directors decided to close it down.

For many this decision put an end to a gentle and reflective part of the school's life and signalled the final, inevitable shift away from the last remnants of an agrarian society. Although the world was, indeed, becoming more mechanized, society had yet to expect highly technical work of its blind, and skills such as those taught at the Trades Department were still in big demand. (It wasn't until World War II that, in order to stay competitive and self-sustaining, students needed a curriculum that included clerical skills such as typing to support the growing office and retail economy.)

Halfway into the second decade of the new century, Oak Hill was growing at an unprecedented rate. The year 1916 saw a bequest of twenty-two thousand dollars from the estate of Mrs. William H. Palmer of Hartford, which provided a much-needed shot in the arm when it increased the institution's endowment to nearly fifty-thousand dollars.

Then on April 28, 1917, the Trades Department moved into a magnificent new building on Ridge Road in Wethersfield, (which is today the home of BESB). The move was a great boon to the Trades Department, which finally had enough room to expand its skills training. That year, the blind adults at the Department turned out 22,865 brooms and 193 whisks, recaned 5,503 chairs, and restuffed 933 mattresses.

Despite the growing endowment, finances were still a great concern. Fortunately, public support of the institution was gradually increasing, and while donations were generally meager (even by the day's standards), the base of support was widening. A list of contributions for the year 1918 range from one dollar from Mrs. J.R. Holly of Bristol to five hundred dollars from Howard B. Tuttle of Naugatuck, with most donations averaging ten dollars.

The year 1918 brought the Armistice that ended the War to End All Wars, along with a worldwide influenza epidemic that claimed twenty million lives.

But in the annals of Oak Hill, the year 1918 was best remembered for another reason. In August of that year, Emily Wells Foster died. Although she suffered with arterial sclerosis for four years before her death, Foster rejoiced that she lived long enough to see the first graduating class leave the school she had established.

School records of the time record a tribute to Foster. Fittingly, it is signed simply, "A Friend." Undoubtedly, there were many among the ranks of students and staff, as well as in the city, who shared the sentiment expressed by the anonymous author:

"Endowed naturally with infinite tenderness and sympathy, she tried to express in her great life work the difference between that charity which doles out aid to unfortunates in a patronizing spirit and that love that bestows its tender care and affection on them as children of our common Father. Hers was the love that could bear and believe and hope and endure all things, not only for the blind but also for other unfortunates who came within the scope of her activities…Having no children of her own, her natural mother love was bestowed on the little blind ones who loved to come to her arms and by whom she was known as 'Foster Mama.' Her memory will ever be blessed by these, many of whom, now in manhood and womanhood, are in a creditable manner doing their share in the world's work."

CHAPTER FOUR

An Emerging  Force

1920 – 1935

As the 1930s broke in the bleak dawn of the Depression, there began to emerge a new era of socially progressive thought.

Oak Hill boys proudly represent Connecticut in an interstate track meet.

Relief maps make geography more meaningful for this boy.

Basketry in the early days.

A private music lesson.

This maple tree, planted by the class of 1927, now towers over the main building.

By the beginning of the third decade of this century, the blind in Connecticut had truly emerged as a social force. In 1921, the state legislature empowered the BESB to authorize home teaching and relief for the "needy blind," and a blind clergyman, the Rev. Edward P. Ayer of Branford, was named chaplain of the Connecticut House of Representatives.

On campus, too, great changes heralded a new life for blind students, who, until then, had encountered widespread, if tacit, prejudice once they ventured too far into sighted society. The school extended its academic curriculum to a full four-year high school course of study, obviating the need for an affiliation with the Perkins Institute.

Like the musical, agricultural and trades training, this important change in the intellectual life of the students is an example of how Oak Hill has been at the forefront of innovation in services to the blind. While part of society still felt the blind should be protected, sheltered and pitied, Oak Hill's philosophy was that self-sufficiency, above all else, was what most benefitted the visually impaired.

It was natural, then, that athletic competition would follow this increase in academic rigor. When Emily Foster first established her nursery, just three decades earlier, most of the children in her care were at first unable to walk because they had never been allowed to try. At Foster's house, they were encouraged "to creep and enjoy the freedom in which other children delight and thrive."[1]

By the 1920s, the blind pupils at Oak Hill had so overcome their fear

---

1. Marshall, George. From an early annual report.

of running in a world they couldn't see that they were routinely competing in — and winning — athletic contests. In 1924, for example, in a track and field event sponsored by the National Athletic Association of Schools for the Blind, the Oak Hill boys won fourth place.

A new bowling alley added to the athletic fervor growing on the campus, and in 1926, physical activity on campus truly came of age with the opening of the Herbert H. White Memorial Gymnasium. This massive new building combined a true gym with an assembly hall and music department with space for recitals. It was named in honor of one of the school's most prominent early supporters and administrators. Herbert White joined the institution's advisory board in 1899 and until his death in 1934 served ably as treasurer and as chairman of the Executive Committee of the Board of Directors.

These were heady days on campus. Photos from that time show these various teams in proud poses, chests bared, hair slicked, some with eyes averted and some staring boldly into the camera for a picture they would never see. In their youthful manliness and bravado, frozen on palladium plates, these boys carry the timeless self-assurance of adolescent boys everywhere. Routinely, they astonished the city by walloping the other local teams.

In ways such as this, Oak Hill's athletic prowess was keeping pace with its growing reputation for academic and rehabilitative excellence. A doctor associated with the Perkins Institute, Edward E. Allen, who was a noted researcher into the methodology of treatment for the blind at the time, frequently cited aspects of the Oak Hill curriculum, including its physical education, as among the most progressive in the world. Referring to a track meet with the Hartford Public High School track team, Allen wrote:

"I once saw a group of (Oak Hill) boys so beat, in track events, a team of boys from the local high school, that as a result, the (Oak Hill) superintendent had no further trouble in getting the gymnasium he wanted. The blind boys' superiority, particularly in the standing high jump, was marked, and in consequence, their seeing competitors, after having done their best, sat down and sheepishly watched the bar raised inch by inch and cleared by those who could only feel how high they were jumping."[2]

As was typical of the times, campus athletic opportunities were limited to the boys; girls were required to take basketry. This is perhaps one of the few times the institution was not progressive in the treatment of its students.

Expansion of the school's physical education programs and

---

2. Allen, Edward E. Quoted in an early annual report.

facilities was spurred on by Gordon C. Hicks, who came on board as superintendent in 1918 when George Marshall stepped down.

Hicks served until 1946 and is remembered by many Oak Hill alumni as a genuinely amiable and kind man who put his dedication to organized sports to work time and again. During his tenure, the school's reputation for athletic excellence continued to grow.

As legendary as Hicks' love of sports was his love of animals, especially large dogs. One fond memory of Hicks belongs to Josephine Pace, whose dedication to the school is known by everyone in the Oak Hill community. Pace graduated in 1951 and taught several semesters at the school beginning in 1955. She then poured her considerable energy into serving as elementary school supervisor, school principal, director of education and, finally, director of group homes. She retired in 1989. Pace says of Hicks:

"He was a really friendly, out-going man who also happened to

SCHOOL SONG

There's a vine-clad nest by a great oak tree
On top of a sunny hill;
When the years are gone and my youth is spent
'Twill cling to my memory still.
When these school-day friends have gone their way
And I face the cares of each dawning day,
Our hearts are still with you dear Oak Hill
And always love you, that we will.

Refrain
To dear O.H.S. we're singing and its tender memory;
Our thoughts are forever winging in a swift happy flight to thee.
And it seems that you stand like a beacon light,
A guide through life's stormy sea;
Oh! Our school on the hill by the old oak tree,
Let us sing lasting praise to thee.

With each passing year comes the memory
Of days that have gone before;
Like the birds in spring and the winter snow,
Could they but return once more,
Then all my cares I would fling away
And rejoice at the dawn of each new-born day;
Our hearts are blessed by you O.H.S.
And by the memories we love best.

Refrain

be quite visually impaired. Whenever he'd walk those big dogs, everybody cleared the way! He had a wonderful sense of humor, which, frankly, horrified his wife. Once a month, she would have these luncheons to which it was considered quite an honor to be invited. One time, around Saint Patrick's Day, she served everything with a 'green theme.' Apparently, Mr. Hicks thought it was a bit

... What our pupils need most to cultivate is that acceptability which accompanies character, personality and power; qualities which come more from how than from what is studied and done at school.

gruesome and said 'It's just as well our guests can't see what they're eating.' She wasn't at all pleased, but we were hysterical."

Athletics were not the only addition to the curriculum during those years. A voice and expression department was added in the late 1920s, along with a "domestic science" course aimed at increasing the pupils' skills at living independently. In a move that did not happen in public schools for years to come, Oak Hill removed some of the earlier gender barriers to foster important skill development. Young boys were introduced to knitting and basketry because teachers discovered these disciplines helped develop the muscle coordination needed in the reading and writing of Braille.

Although the Nursery and School Departments were growing rapidly and broadening their scope, the Trades Department was

beginning to feel a decline. The mainstays of the industrial work were losing popularity with the public. Rag rugs and reed furniture were being replaced in consumers' homes with imports and woven fibers. As the Great Depression loomed, the Trades Department struggled valiantly to keep its head above water economically, experimenting with other industries, such as the splitting of rattan for brooms and the stuffing of toys for mass consumption. Although no one recognized it at the time, the impending demise of the Trades Department would, in the long run, be good for the school and its pupils, as it signalled the beginning of a newer, more intellectual, place for the blind in the labor market.

As the 1930s broke in the bleak dawn of the Depression, there began to emerge a new era of socially progressive thought. One sign of this trend toward enlightenment was the election, in 1930, of Connecticut's beloved governor Wilbur Cross, who would go on to win three more gubernatorial elections. Cross, known for his social liberalism and great oratorical style, was an ardent supporter of Oak Hill. Cross opened the 40th Anniversary exercises in 1933, at which Antonio Martone delighted the audience with a piano solo, Reinhold's *Impromptu in G Sharp Minor*, as well as a violin solo, Mendelssohn's *Andante*.

On campus, progressive thought ruled the day, as educators and medical experts alike agreed on the wisdom of emphasizing the individual over the masses, and each person's potential over his shortcomings. Edward Allen was one of the progressive education movement's progenitors. Allen argued eloquently against the "shut-in provincialized pupil," and in so doing, was probably one of the first advocates of what we call "mainstreaming" today.

Although he advanced this radical theory in a town known for its provincialism, Allen found many kindred spirits at Oak Hill, who applauded his theories and, indeed, carried them out by continually expanding the school's curriculum and honoring the "intimate environmental training" he encouraged. Arguing for the need to send well-prepared blind students forth to classes in regular public schools, Allen said: "Such a scheme would seem to require continuing the common curriculum, however, and, as you know, progressive education breaks away from this conformity and adapts...to the individual child...What our pupils need most to cultivate is that acceptability which accompanies character, personality and power; qualities which come more from *how* than from *what* is studied and done at school."[3]

Even as American educators such as Allen and his Oak Hill colleague Herbert White were advancing the rights of the individual in society, Adolf Hitler was made German Chancellor and began to lay the groundwork for his Third Reich. The peaceful, progressive school had no inkling of the war that lay ahead.

By 1935, enrollment had risen to sixty-five in the School Department alone, making it the largest enrollment yet. Over the next few decades, Oak Hill would continue to grow by leaps and bounds, reflecting a more stable financial base, a growing constituency and an increasingly progressive philosophy that remains the lifeblood of the institution.

On January 24, 1935, four years before the outbreak of World War II, a devastating fire completely destroyed the Farmington nursery. Although none of the eighteen children in residence or staff members was injured, the fire swept everyone at Oak Hill up in its terror and devastation.

Gert DeLeo, who was a teenager at the time, remembered that cool heads prevailed amid the catastrophe. She was pressed into duty that freezing night when Lil-

---

3. Ibid.

lian Russell and her assistant Edna Joslyn (known to all as "Mama Jo") tried to account for all the children and get them to safety.

"We stood there in the dark," DeLeo recalled. "My job was to tell them whether each child was a boy or a girl, so they could separate them appropriately. I remember holding onto little Joe Kisiel and saying 'He's only a baby — can't he come on our side?' Josephine Pace, who was about three at the time, was crying, so I took her to bed with me. I will never forget that night. They were all in their pajamas and their hair smelled of smoke…"

Raking hay into "windrows…"

PLANTING & TUMBLING

Eight of the boys were assigned garden plots...(each) doing the greater part of the work himself. These young gardeners were perfectly delighted with their new occupation, spending most of their spare time in their gardens; first thing in the morning and last thing at night you would find them there. The long dry spell had no terrors for them. Their gardens were never thirsty and there was no lack of cultivation. They were stirring up the earth most of the time.

The first one to find something peeping through the ground was hailed as a hero, and there was a lively stampede to see the rare phenomenon, and a lingering suspicion exists that some of the tender shoots were so much overcome by such an abundance of worldly curiosity that they never quite recovered.

When the lettuce and radishes were large enough to use, proud, indeed, was the youngster whose privilege it was to supply the table with the product of his labor.

These gardens contained a little of everything, for the children were allowed considerable latitude as to what they might plant...Some mistakes were made at first, plants being pulled up for weeds but, on the whole, such mistakes were few; the boys very quickly learned to distinguish between vegetables and weeds by the texture and shape of the leaves. Some of those who had a little sight made more blunders in this respect than those without any vision. The former depended too much upon the little sight they possessed while the latter relied on their well trained sense of touch...

The hay-making afforded nearly as much enjoyment as the gardening; it was such fun to rake the new-mown hay into cocks for the night; spread it out again in the morning, or rake it into windrows and tumble...

— George Marshall

The Years of

War & Peace

1936 – 1959

The presence or absence of faith was a particularly resonant theme in America during those years, when the Depression cloaked virtually every aspect of the nation's life in a sense of collective and individual failure. But at Oak Hill, revolutionary educational methods were continuing to astound even the most skeptical pundits and encouraged the students' faith in themselves and in their school.

Oak Hill girls take part in the on-campus athletics.

The graduating class of 1938.

Oak Hill boys show their athletic prowess on the parallel bars, circa 1945.

Oak Hill athletes use guide wires as they run to glory in track competitions.

Piano tuning in the 1950s.

Smoke may have been in their hair, but not in their eyes. Instinctively, the Oak Hill students, staff and administration saw through the fire's devastation to the potential that lay beneath the wreckage. Although homeless for three years, moving from one temporary headquarters to another, by 1938 the Nursery Department was in full swing again. That year, Oak Hill opened Founders House, home of the new Nursery and Kindergarten named in honor of Emily Foster and Lillian Russell.

On the west wall of Founders House there is a plaque which reads: "We Walk by Faith, Not by Sight." It is a fitting tribute, but not only because it was faith that compelled the institution's founders to persevere against social ignorance, legislative indifference, the Depression and the uncertainty inherent in all philanthropy. These words are fitting for another, perhaps more important, reason: throughout the school's history, its students have relied on the faith in oneself that makes all people strong.

In one hundred years, the faces passing through Oak Hill's doors have been as diverse as any school or college could claim. They have run the gamut of intellectual ability, physical prowess, talent, racial origin, religious affiliation, political leaning and temperament. And yet they share something crucial: the belief that sightlessness is nothing compared to faithlessness.

The presence or absence of faith was a particularly resonant theme in America during those years, when the Depression cloaked virtually every aspect of the nation's life in a sense of collective and individual failure. But at Oak Hill, revolutionary educational methods were continuing to astound even the most skeptical pundits and encouraged the students' faith in themselves and in their school.

One innovation concerned writing Braille with a stylus. Traditionally, blind students wrote by inserting a paper into a hinged brass slate on which were embossed a series of dots arranged in groupings of six, known as cells. The students would line up the pointed stylus with the dot formation for the desired letter and then puncture the paper. Because this was, in essence, a negative or reverse image of the letter, the children were forced to write backwards. They would then flip the slate left to right in order to read what they had written. Oak Hill educators, however, discovered that by flipping the slate top to bottom, before the writing, the child could write and read left to right.

The results of this methodology, along with similar innovations, were impressive. In 1943, BESB conducted a comprehensive study of the last quarter century of the school's life. Of the seventy-two students who had attended, fully a quarter had gone on to higher education and 90 percent of the graduates were self-supporting at a time when the national unemployment rate was still unprecedented.

The war years, which were proving to be such an economic boon to the nation, stimulated life at the Trades Department, too. Over the years, the Trades Department had become more a sheltered workshop than a true training school. (This shift really began in the 1920s, when BESB, following a national trend, began to teach trades in the home.) During the war, however, business was booming at the corner of Ridge Road and Jordan Lane; the Trades Department's blind adult workers made and shipped a whopping 242,300 pillow cases to the U.S. armed forces abroad. For the public, the Department made 19,512 brooms and recaned 1,267 chairs.

While the war had temporarily boosted the demand for Trades Department goods, the operation was still not economically feasible: an annual report of the time reveals that the yearly cost of running the Trades Department was one hundred and thirty thousand dollars. Of this amount, twelve thousand dollars was paid for by state workshop fees and board and tuition costs and another thirty-five thousand was grossed from the broom, chair and mat sales. This left an eighty-three-thousand-dollar deficit to be paid for out of the institution's endowment. In years to come, this would prove too prohibitive.

During the war, however, the blind clients of the institution's Trades Department were as caught up in patriotic fervor as any other non-commissioned American "war worker."

Students on campus, who for years had been perfecting their "hand work," knit and rolled bandages far faster and more efficiently than did sighted volunteers.

While the war years did not change much at the school, they do give context to the students' experience. Too often, the blind are thought of as isolated from the reality of sighted society, when, in fact, these students were not so different from other Americans during that terrifying, (and ultimately jubilant) time. The interior, emotional landscape for the blind student was much the same as that of the sighted child. Here, blindness affected only how the information was being processed, not what information, or why.

While sighted children, inculcated with fear of the enemy, were shown frightening filmstrips to remind them to "duck and cover," the blind students were receiving the same message audibly.

"The worst part were the air raid drills," recalls Josephine Pace. "I remember those awful sirens screeching above our heads. With blind people, because you depend so much more on your hearing, the effect of all that noise was terrifying. I think it was our inability to hear directions clearly that scared us so as kids. We would go and hide under our beds and in closets. Our school building had a siren for the whole area, and when I say the air raids were loud, God Almighty, the building vibrated."

Nationally, significant changes were occurring that would affect the lives of blind people throughout the world. In 1942, Dr. Samuel Hayes of Mount Holyoke College developed a radical new method of testing the intellectual potential of the blind. This adaptation of the popular Stanford-Binet intelligence test, called the Hayes-Binet Test, served to dispel lingering doubts that visual impairment necessarily implied mental impairment. Its invention marked a new era of societal sensitivity to physical handicaps.

"Just as had World War I, the Second World War had a profound affect on the lives of the blind in America," according to Kenneth Stuckey, research librarian at The Perkins Institute. "Here was another group of veterans returning home without the ability to see. And like their World War I predecessors, they made new demands on society, which in turn became more aware of the needs of the blind."

One critical advancement during this time, Stuckey says, was the 'long cane,' or Hoover Technique of mobility, developed by Dr. Richard Hoover of the Maryland School for the Blind. The vast expansion of public transportation, too, opened up opportunities for the blind; a good piano tuner, for example, could visit clients far from home, and thereby make a better living for himself.

In addition, skills such as transcribing from a dictaphone or operating a switchboard, opened up new opportunities for the blind in the workforce, especially women.

In 1944, as the Allies turned the tide of the war with the Normandy Invasion, the city of Hartford experienced "the Day the Clowns Cried" — a tragedy of such monumental proportion that for many it remains, fifty years later, the city's darkest hour. The Barnum and Bailey circus fire, which took 168 lives, lingers in the memories of some CIB alumni who were children at the time. Just as did the ravages of war, the circus fire proved that tears of rage and grief issue just as freely from the eyes of the blind.

Although it is believed that none of the students lost a loved one in that fire, alumni remember the temporary first aid station Oak Hill set up and offered to rescue workers. "I don't recall it was ever actually used," says Josephine Pace, "but all of us students were well aware of the gravity of the situation; we were all moved about to make room."

Two years later, with the fires at home and abroad for the most part extinguished, Oak Hill's administrators noticed a marked dip in enrollment. While most institutions dread this sort of news, for a school specializing in services to the blind, this phenomenon is a mixed blessing. All true philanthropists dream of a day when their services are obsolete and the Oak Hill family would undoubtedly rejoice on that unlikely day.

But clearly, blindness was far from eradicated. So in the late 1940s, as enrollments reached an all-time low of thirty-eight pupils (as compared to the seventy-one students enrolled just a decade earlier), Frank Johns, who had become superintendent in 1946 upon the retirement of Gordon Hicks, determined to find out why. After studying the situation, Johns reported three root causes for the decline: many older students had left for wartime employment, sight-saving classes in public schools had become more popular and effective, and medical advances had helped to prevent or reduce some forms of blindness.

From the institution's founding, Oak Hill educators were well acquainted with the reasons for blindness. In Emily Foster's day, "babies' sore eyes" was the homey term used for ophthalmia neonatorum, an inflammation in the eyes of newborns who were exposed to a gonorrheal bacterium during delivery.

Because Victorian society shunned any discussion of venereal diseases, ophthalmia neonatorum accounted for at least 30 percent of all cases of blindness. This is especially tragic given that doctors knew fairly early on that they could prevent the disease simply by dropping silver nitrate into the newborn's eyes.

But because such social taboos persisted well into this century, it wasn't until a few crusading doctors and educators (among them Helen Keller) forced the issue that state governments began to insist the medical establishment pay attention to the crisis. A twenty-year educational effort paid off and today, cases of the disease are extremely rare; silver nitrate drops are now routinely administered to all babies born in American hospitals. In her early years of ministering to young children, Emily Foster contracted babies' sore eyes from her first pupil, Antonio Martello, whom she found in the tenement. Foster was cured of the illness in Boston, and Martello became "Tony the Blind Newsboy" — the respected newsstand proprietor on Hartford's Union Place.

Syphilis, too, took its toll on newborn infants in the institution's early years, as did tuberculosis, smallpox and scarlet and typhoid fevers. The significance of these diseases as causes of blindness has slowly waned. In the mid 1960s, a

AN ABUNDANCE OF VOLUNTEERS

There is a natural joy that exists between teachers and students; they give to one another and take from one another in a perfect symbiosis. For a volunteer who works on behalf of a school, that joy is less visible, although no less real. In its one-hundred-year history, Oak Hill has known thousands of such volunteers whose joy lies solely in the giving.

Some are individual men and women who feel compelled to give of themselves to the place — people like Mr. and Mrs. Robert Roth, whose family foundation provides each student on campus with a birthday celebration. Others are children who look at the Oak Hill students and see, along with the differences, enough of themselves to know instinctively how to help.

And finally, much philanthropic largesse comes from groups of civic-minded people who band together for a common cause. One such organization was the Ladies Visiting Committee, whose existence, for decades, was inextricably bound with the life of the school itself.

While the efforts of many such committees get lost in the shuffle of running a non-profit organization, no one associated with Oak Hill could ever overlook the efficacy and generosity of this group of volunteers.

For years, the Ladies Visiting Committee gave hundreds of gifts and stockings to children who were unable to be with their own families at Christmas. Members of the Committee helped establish the Lions Gallery of the Senses at the Wadsworth Atheneum and helped mobilize numerous local philanthropic groups on the school's behalf. The Ladies Visiting Committee also raised thousands of dollars for the building of the school's swimming and recreation facility.

One longtime member, Mary Morton, still visits Thompson House in Newington each week to read to the residents there. Many dedicated women have poured their considerable talent and energy into the activities of the Committee. However, in addition to Mary Morton, two women must be singled out for their tireless dedication. Mary Pope Cheney and Lucy T. Mink led their colleagues on the Committee in providing both the physical and moral support all effective organizations need.

But volunteer spirit at Oak Hill is hardly limited to the Ladies Visiting Committee. A plethora of local civic groups has donated time, talent and considerable resources through the years. In 1992, one group, the Hartford Lions Club, marked its forty-ninth year of providing holiday luncheons and gifts to the Oak Hill students.

Several other groups have giving histories that span decades. The Teamsters Local 599, for example, has given holiday parties and visits from Santa for more than twenty years. The Sisterhood of Beth Hillel Synagogue has spent twenty-five years rigging up a spooky Halloween party and the Telephone Pioneers of America have rolled out an Easter egg hunt, complete with easy-to-find beeping eggs, for more than twenty springs.

Many other local groups, including schools, radio stations, state agencies, religious institutions and private corporations have worked quietly behind the scenes to make life more fun for the Oak Hill students.

One of Mary Cheney's favorite quotations, from Goethe, sums up the spirit of these varied and generous groups:

"I see with a feeling eye, I feel with a seeing hand."

Of these volunteers, one might reasonably add that they do, with their hands and hearts, what others only imagine doing.

national rubella (German measles) epidemic caused about thirty thousand children to be born with various birth defects, among which were about six thousand cases of blindness.[1] By the late 1960s and early 1970s, nearly 15 percent of Oak Hill's cases of blindness were attributed to diabetes, and the same amount to glaucoma. As always, a certain percent were caused by hereditary and congenital conditions, as well as by accidents.

But beginning in the early 1940s, just as enrollment was declining, an epidemic was brewing that would, by the time it crested in the early 1950s, cause Oak Hill's numbers to swell again. Retrolental fibroplasia is a medical fairy tale turned nightmare.

In the 1940s, as advances in medical technology grew exponentially, science was able for the first time to save infants born three and four months premature. Tragically, for as many as one of every four of these infants, the loss of sight accompanied this miraculous birth like a stranger at a wedding.

It would be nearly two decades before researchers understood that the simple administration of too much oxygen to these "preemies" would cause, at some later stage, the growth of fibrous tumors behind the eye's lens. By then, as many as twelve thousand children in this country were blinded by well-meaning, but ignorant, medical personnel. One particularly sad aspect of this story is that in some hospitals, compassionate nurses unwittingly thwarted the efforts of some doctors who, getting close to discovering the cause of the outbreak, experimented with lower oxygen doses:

"Cutting down on oxygen was much easier said than done," wrote Dr. Arnall Patz, one of the doctors studying the epidemic. "The night nurses were always turning (the oxygen) on again because they were so sure we were doing wrong. And it was a tough thing to

1. Koestler, Frances A. From *The Unseen Minority* (David McKay Co., 1976)

sleep with, this business of keeping babies on low oxygen when all the teaching had been to give them plenty of it."[2]

By 1951, Johns reported, retrolental fibroplasia accounted for more than half of all new students at Oak Hill. And by 1955, enrollment was at an all-time high of 110 students, double that of just five years earlier.

Long before this time, Oak Hill's remarkable contributions to society were widely evident and undisputed. So when the school's administration needed to convince the legislature to appropriate funds for more space and services, they had a much easier time of it than did their forebears. In 1954, the state government approved an additional $345,000 for new dormitories and classrooms at Oak Hill. Although a great boost to the school's budget, the appropriation would not cover the increases in annual operating expenses, and so

that same year, the school's Board of Directors instituted an annual fund drive.

The next year, another change at the State Capitol would have a profound effect on life at Oak Hill. Legislation was passed to allow all blind children in the state to attend public school at the State's expense.

This radical law validated Oak Hill's long-standing credo that the blind should participate in sighted society as much as possible. At the same time, however, it diminished the significance of blindness as a reason to attend a special school. In the 1950s, Oak Hill began to encourage students in its upper classes to spend most or all of their senior year in the high school of their home districts so they could, technically, graduate from that school. When this was not feasible logistically, Oak Hill students attended nearby Weaver High School in Hartford, and earned their diplomas from that public school.

Trends such as this, along with

the new legislation, laid the groundwork for a significant shift in the focus of Oak Hill's work. Although this change would not really come into play until the late 1960s, it was becoming clear that Oak Hill was broadening its scope of services and that the profile of the student body was a changing one.

Any significant change in education or social work must, of course, be looked at in the local, national and global context of its time. This was the era of Khrushchev, Sputnik, the hydrogen bomb, the Bay of Pigs, the Berlin Wall. It was the birth of the space race and the Peace Corps. It was the terrifying winds of Hurricane Carol. But it was also the gentle winds blowing across the fields at Camp Harkness, the school's gift to the children of the 1950s, who watched as world events rapidly eroded their innocence.

In a seventy-five-year retrospective written in 1968 by staff member Martha Hancock, "change, progress and achievement" were the

2. Ibid.

61

This was the era of Khrushchev, Sputnik, the hydrogen bomb, the Bay of Pigs, the Berlin Wall. It was the birth of the space race and the Peace Corps. It was the terrifying winds of Hurricane Carol. But it was also the gentle winds blowing across the fields at Camp Harkness, the school's gift to the children of the 1950s, who watched as world events rapidly eroded their innocence.

signposts of this era in the school's history. By the early 1960s, Oak Hill teachers found themselves serving a rapidly changing student body. Where historically the school was made up of pupils whose only limitation was blindness or visual impairment, more and more of the Oak Hill young people had multiple disabilities.

"The emerging trends and distinctive directions that mark[ed] this particular growth period are revealed in several developments," Hancock wrote. "In the School Department, the percentage of multiple-handicapped students rose rapidly. In order to care for the total needs of these students, services of an even more highly specialized nature than were already being offered became a necessity."

One manifestation of this change is the medical treatment needed to serve the students adequately. As late as the 1940s, annual eye checks, inoculations and the occasional tonsillectomy made up the bulk of the necessary medical attention. But by the 1950s, Superintendent Frank Johns saw the growing need to introduce on-campus nurses, physical and occupational therapists, speech therapists, neurologists and psychologists.

So rapidly was the student body changing, in fact, that by 1965, a psychiatric-neurological survey revealed that approximately 75 percent of the students had disabilities in addition to blindness, with 15 percent having three or more such additional disabilities.

The tone of this report, as related in annual reports of the time, is matter-of-fact and accepting. This history is significant, for while other institutions might have resisted or lamented so dramatic a change in their role, Oak Hill responded with characteristic determination and willingness to change with the needs of its children.

A winter romp on Holcomb Street, circa 1955.

CAMP HARKNESS

By the mid 1950s, Oak Hill, like much of the nation, was moving rapidly toward an ethos of personal liberation that would come to fruition in the 1960s. One manifestation of this new freedom was the increased emphasis on physical expression and exploration, especially through athletics and outdoor activities. Far from sheltered or protected, Oak Hill girls competed in an annual track meet sponsored by the Eastern Athletic Association for the Blind, and Oak Hill boys wrestled their way to personal "stardom" in interscholastic tournaments. There were also Boy Scout and Girl Scout troops established at the school, as well as 4-H programs. (So challenging was the coordination of these burgeoning programs that the Oak Hill administration soon created the position of Director of Recreation.)

Popular as sporting events were, the most popular and longlasting of the new physical activities was Camp Harkness, a summer camping program that took full advantage of the serene beauty of Harkness Memorial State Park in Waterford.

Established in 1959 with just eighteen campers, the camp was begun quietly, almost experimentally, by campus teachers and counselors. But by 1965, more than eighty students each year were able to enjoy the camaraderie and freedom the camp offered.

The therapeutic benefits of Camp Harkness were immediately evident and each year, the popularity of the camp grew with both students and staff. Today, the camp is for many the high point of the year's recreational activities.

Craig Cody, 31, is one Oak Hill person who does not need to be prodded into expounding upon the benefits of Camp Harkness. Craig, who has cerebral palsy, first became an Oak Hill student in 1962 and now lives in an Oak Hill community residence with five other people in Hartland.

"Camp Harkness is one great thing out of many great things at Oak Hill," Craig says. "They have fabulous volunteers there who help a client do anything he wants. They take us swimming, and on the swings, on field trips and out to eat at this gorgeous pavilion. The camp is right on the ocean and it's so very peaceful there."

When asked to sum up his feelings about Camp Harkness, Craig pauses thoughtfully and says, "There, I feel right at home."

Graduates gather at a recent reunion at Camp Harkness.

Craig Cody and group home manager Karla Lindquist share a joke at the one hundredth anniversary kick-off in the spring of 1993.

"Oak Hill has always been progressive and in the forefront of new trends in treatment," says Josephine Pace. "We've never waited for others to lead the way. There are numerous examples of this: getting blind and deaf kids involved in the community, mainstreaming students in the 1950s into regular public high schools, creating one of the nation's first deaf/blind education departments in 1969 and experimental educational methods, such as the Braille writing reversal.

"And then, with the increase in low-functioning deaf/blind students, all the nation's experts were arguing about what to do and how to do it. Nobody wanted to handle them, but we just jumped in and said 'We'll do it.' And we kept at it until we found a way to make it work."

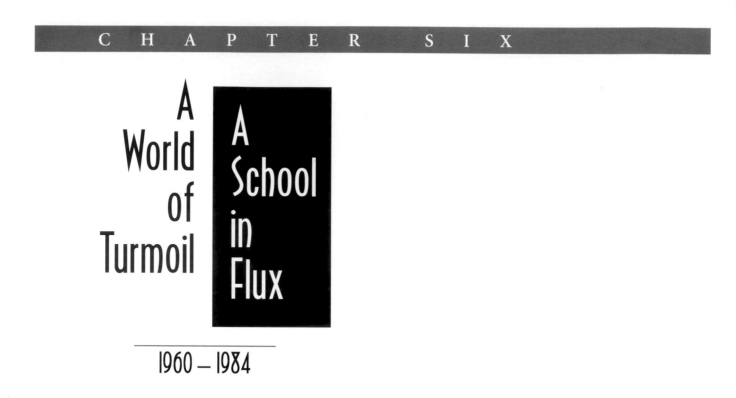

A
World
of
Turmoil

A
School
in
Flux

1960 – 1984

This landmark legislation made all the difference in special education because it guaranteed all children free, appropriate public education in the least restrictive environment possible.

Dr. Lars Guldager.

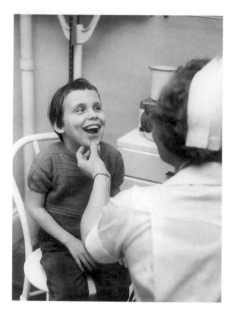

Regular check-ups keep Oak Hill children healthy.

Everyday skills are a constant concern for the blind students of the 1950s.

The wading pool doubles as a skating rink for two young friends.

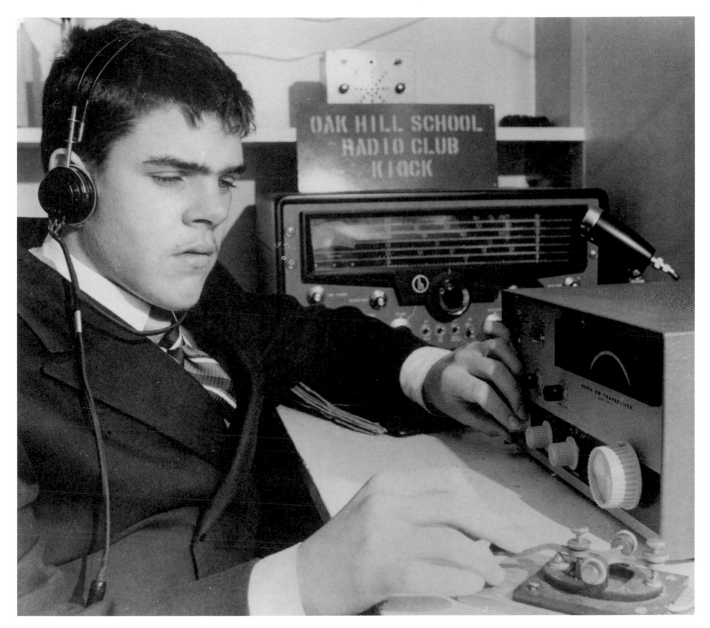

An Oak Hill boy learns how to operate a ham radio.

Former Governor John Dempsey visits an Oak Hill typing class in the early 1960s.

change was indeed becoming the lifeblood of Oak Hill. Fittingly, changes in the school's educational methods, classroom procedures and social work were, in themselves, revolutionary at a time when revolution was the order of the day everywhere else. In this fascinating period in American history, the naive and placid post-war city and nation were jolted into the turbulent "adolescence" of the 1960s. Across the country, mounting racial tensions, the escalating Vietnam war and generational rifts rent families and communities apart; increasingly, people focussed on their differences and not on what they shared as a people. On the Oak Hill campus, however, there was a growing sense of unity, because here, the emphasis was on ability, not disability, and on shared experience rather than isolation.

One good example of this is the question of race relations and the ways in which segregation affected the education of young people. This was the time of the Greensboro protests and the march on Selma. Blacks who tried to attend public (white) schools were frequently imprisoned or murdered instead. In Hartford, just a mile from the Oak Hill campus, long stretches of Albany Avenue ignited, smoldered and then flared as tempers did.

Because mass society is inclined to oversimplify the causes of strife, there are times when blindness is glorified. We like to think that if "justice is blind," we are objective, and that if "love is blind," we are tolerant (although perhaps slightly delusionary). Prejudice, however, is anything but blind; the ability to *see* black, or brown or white skin makes all the difference in race relations.

But at Oak Hill, it seemed that if one's eyes were blind to skin color, it followed that one's heart was, too. And while campuses throughout the city, the state and the nation agonized over racial unrest, the students at Oak Hill went about the business of living and learning together in harmony just as they had done from the very early days, when Martello and Martone were considered the names of minorities.

By now the effects of the retrolental fibroplasia epidemic were dramatic; Oak Hill's enrollments remained at an all-time high. In addition, a new kind of student was joining the Oak Hill family. The rubella outbreak of the mid 1960s sent dozens of deaf and blind young people through the doors years later when they reached school age.

The trend toward enrolling children with multiple disabilities signalled a bold new direction for the school and heralded a crucial new resource for the social and medical communities. Previously, young people with such disabilities would most likely have been institutionalized or cared for at home by ill-equipped guardians. As Oak Hill's expertise in this field expanded, however, educators, doctors and social service personnel from throughout the country sought placement at the school for their increasing numbers of such students.

About this time, groups of Oak Hill teachers began developing curriculum guides, and here, too, Oak Hill's expertise was of national renown.

"Up until that time, there was very little available information on low-functioning deaf and blind students, and textbooks for them were quite inadequate," recalls Josephine Pace. "We began to write curriculum guides that followed the usual subjects, running the gamut from English and social studies to math and science, but adapted for deaf/blind use. People sent for them in droves."

The reason these guides were so effective is that they were written by the true experts — not educational theorists, but rather, the teachers who spent hours each day with children with severe disabilities. By taking nothing for granted except the child's need to learn and the teacher, therapist or parent's desire to help, the guides have helped thousands of caregivers work with children with special needs.

In writing the guides, the teachers took a practical, step-by-step approach to physical and intellectual tasks. They recognized that even the simplest act, such as climbing stairs, can take enormous dedication on the part of both teacher and student. The language is simple and unadorned, but the insight derives from years of experience in the field of special education.

The year 1965 was a pivotal one in the history of Oak Hill. Acting upon a long-held belief that the Trades Department had outlived its usefulness, the Board of Directors voted to shut it down. When Frank Cleaveland formed the Trades Department in the late 1800s, it was a bold step. For the first time, blind citizens were not objects of pity or scorn, but productive members of the labor market. Because of the Trades Department's proud history, many saw its demise as a sad moment in the life of the institution.

But because at Oak Hill nostalgia is kept in check by innovation, the end of the Trades Depart-

FROM A TEACHER'S POINT OF VIEW

Excerpted from A Practical Guide to the Training of Low-functioning Deaf-Blind Children, *written in 1973 by Oak Hill teachers Marcia J. Watson and Judith L. Nicholas.*

Mastering the Stairs: Up

1. Children at Oak Hill must go up and down stairs several times a day. If your child does not, do not urge stair mastery until he is very steady on his feet.
2. Many children will naturally try to crawl up the stairs.
3. Climbing the steps of a small slide with much help is a good preliminary to climbing stairs.
4. Use a banister the child can hold onto well.
5. Have the child hold the banister with one hand while you hold his other hand.
6. Push his banister hand forward, lifting the same foot to the next step for him. (If he naturally lifts the other foot, that is fine, too.)
7. Pull his other hand, lifting the corresponding foot.
8. Repeat the procedure (5-7) to the landing.
9. The next time he encounters stairs, repeat for a few stairs, then touch the foot he is to lift, lifting it for him only if he cannot do it by himself.
10. When he will lift his feet without prodding, touch his banister hand without pushing it, so he will learn to pull on the banister alone.
11. As he practices climbing the stairs and does better, acting more confident, let go of his hand, urging him to go alone. If he will not, touch his hand, standing ahead of him to encourage him. A shining flashlight or a toy ahead of him can cause some children to walk up the stairs for it.

ment era was looked upon as a great victory, too. The Oak Hill family rejoiced in the significance of the closing: society had become so much more accepting of the blind as a class that their role in the general labor market was far more sophisticated — and profitable — than it had been when the Trades Department was first established. No longer relegated to manual labor of broommaking and chair caning, the blind graduates of Oak Hill had more intellectually stimulating pursuits in fields such as counseling, computers, education, music and social work.

In addition, unlike the rest of the school, the Department had not really changed with the times, and its self-imposed obsolescence proved to be its undoing in an institution that thrived on progress. And now, with the increasing numbers of pupils with multiple disabilities, the work of the Trades Department was at the

same time too simple for some and too complicated for others.

As the rest of the country continued to struggle with the assassinations of its heroes, the human and financial toll of Vietnam and the continuing rift between parent and child, Oak Hill had reason to celebrate. Despite the sense of national psychic drain, the school rejoiced in its ever-expanding curriculum. In 1966, the school's first summer session was launched.

This change began a new era at Oak Hill; by creating a twelve-month program, the school was meeting a need expressed increasingly by parents of children with severe disabilities. By providing

*P*rejudice, however, is anything but blind; the ability to see *black, or brown or white skin makes all the difference in race relations.*

continual, intensive programs, Oak Hill was affording its students a continuum of care.

Again, this was seen as a radical departure from the past, in which young people with severe disabilities lived in large institutions and were not generally considered educable.

In 1965, an important new building was added to the campus. It was named for Rockwell Harmon Potter, who had resigned in 1957 as Board president after serving his fifty-year term. His duties as Board president were assumed by Dr. Harvey K. McArthur, faculty emeritus and former acting president of Hartford Seminary. During his tenure, Potter was a staunch advocate for the rights of the blind to an education equal to that of sighted students. Potter Hall, whose design was predicated entirely on the needs of the blind student, was built at a cost of $475,000. There, pupils learned to tune pianos, to cook for themselves, to work with metal, to type and

74

to master many physical and intellectual skills.

Several other new buildings greatly augmented Oak Hill's ability to serve its expanding student body. The Library Center, complete with an audio resource room, opened in 1967 and the popular Swimming and Recreation Building was added to the campus in 1969. This latter building was a great victory for the Ladies Visiting Committee, which had been working for years to raise the necessary funds.

The year 1967 saw the retirement of McArthur, who was replaced as Board president by yet another Hartford Seminary figure, the Rev. Robert Edwards. Edwards, a well-respected local historian and author, was at the time the pastor of the Immanuel Congregational Church in Hartford.

About this time, the financial picture at Oak Hill changed somewhat with an important change in the federal law concerning the education of children with disabilities. Title I of the Elementary and Secondary Education Act, enacted in 1965, freed up considerable grant money for purposes such as summer school programs, library equipment and curriculum development.

Other services and programs conducted by Oak Hill have garnered national and even international kudos. In the late 1960s, BESB created a college preparatory program involving mobility training, everyday independent living skills and study skills. (Frequently, blind students find these skills harder to adapt to on a regular college campus than the academic work itself, and so require extra help before beginning the semester.) Four Boston College students lived for a time on the Oak Hill campus while they participated in the BESB program there.

By the 1960s, the Oak Hill students were becoming increasingly visible in the community. The school was frequently asked to visit civic and church groups so the public could gain a better understanding of blindness. Tours on the campus were in constant demand, too. Because many of its students were venturing into the community as many as three and four times each week at the request of these groups, in 1963 the school hired an independent filmmaker to shoot a movie that could be sent in lieu of the students. "The White Cane" was used for years to raise public consciousness about people with disabilities.

Another event occurred in the late 1960s which, like the movie, was an important symbol of the blind students' growing independence. Three students and two of their teachers took a two-month bicycle trip through Europe under the aegis of the American Youth Hostels. Upon their return, the intrepid travelers were greeted with all sorts of demands for speaking engagements because they presented "a new image of blind persons emerging into fuller participation in experiences traditionally denied to them because of obstacles, either real or imagined."[1]

---

1. Hancock, Martha. *The First Seventy-five Years,* CIB, 1968.

In 1976, just as the student body was, as stated before, becoming increasingly multi-handicapped, two crucial changes came in the life of Oak Hill.

First, the federal government enacted two major laws which furthered the cause of all students with disabilities, but especially of those who were profoundly retarded or neurologically impaired.

Public Law 94-142, along with Section 504 of the Vocational Rehabilitation Act, bolstered a ground-breaking ruling in Connecticut a decade earlier which provided special education services to all state school children in need of them. This landmark legislation made all the difference in special education because it guaranteed all children free, appropriate public education in the least restrictive environment possible. In effect, it flung open the door to mainstreaming and bore out the beliefs of Oak Hill educators.

Secondly, Executive Director Lars Guldager came on board, replacing Frank Johns, who was retiring. Guldager, who had been an administrator of special education in the Massachusetts public schools and coordinator of the New England Regional Center for Deaf-Blind Children, took Oak Hill's tradition of bucking the tide and pushed it to the limit. Born in Denmark and educated and employed both there and in the United States, Guldager soon showed a taste for broad-based, open-minded and progressive treatment of children with disabilities.

Children who, in addition to blindness or visual impairment also had disabilities such as mental retardation or severe health involvement, demonstrated to him the greatest need for service.

"It's quite simple," Guldager says in his direct, engaging way, "we took the kids no other educators wanted. Children were stuck away in nursing homes simply because they were retarded. They got virtually no stimulation there and so they just languished. I think that's criminal. And because we talk 'normalization' here, we don't think people who are retarded are all that different when it comes to the things that make us all happy. They need to be clothed, fed, taught, respected and loved. So that's what we do."

This mission, so succinctly stated, got a push from the new federal laws enacted in 1976 because they assured that children with disabilities have the right to education with peers who don't have disabilities. As a result, blind children with no other significant disabilities (the kind of student traditionally enrolled at Oak Hill until the 1970s) could now be expected to attend public school with sighted children.

It was at this point that BESB and Oak Hill defined for themselves clearly divergent paths; BESB would take care of the state's blind students and support efforts to mainstream them, while Oak Hill would care for students with multiple disabilities whose needs were too great for regular schools at that time.

After extensive study and consultation with state care providers,

Guldager laid the groundwork for Oak Hill to serve young people with visual impairment and other disabilities that ranged from mild to profound retardation, and in 1976 Oak Hill enrolled its first students referred from the State Department of Mental Retardation.

By 1986, CIB had amended its articles of incorporation and bylaws to enable the school officially to serve people with disabilities which did not necessarily include visual impairment. Expanding the school's mission in this way more accurately reflected the changing needs of society.

Because serving people with severe disabilities demands aggressive treatment, Oak Hill responded with innovative curriculum development. Special emphasis was placed on personal care skills, social adjustment and work skills, in addition to the more traditional academic work for those who were capable of it. The Work Experience Program, the Deaf-Blind Program and an expanded Industrial Arts Curriculum all met the needs

Sign language opens up communication between this student and her teacher.

of these children and young adults.

As Oak Hill broadened its expertise in the field of curriculum development and training for people with multiple disabilities, the institution's reputation expanded, too. Because the greater part of compassionate care may lie in sharing one's expertise, Oak Hill did this freely and with great results.

It continued to develop and distribute its curriculum guides and special guides for parents, such as *Let's Try to Help: A Guide for Parents of Young Multihandicapped Children,* which proved to be a godsend to hundreds of parents in need of help.

This time in the institution's history also saw the production of several more films featuring Oak Hill's life and programs, which fur-

77

Adaptive equipment and modern technology help this youngster learn and communicate.

ther spread the good word about the institution's innovative treatment of children with disabilities. In 1977, Oak Hill produced the important training film "Mobility in Action." Another film, "Oak Hill Makes it Happen," was produced in 1981 by Audrey and Kevin Donovan, who later became corporators of CIB. "Oak Hill Makes it Happen" was seen worldwide by special education experts. In 1984, the Donovans made the film "From Now On," which gave insight into the life of community living for people with disabilities.

As Oak Hill moved further into the 1980s, it was becoming clear that additional staff were needed to care for these students with complex disabilities. Always striving to maintain a workable teacher/student ratio, the school added several teachers, physical, occupational, speech and music therapists and medical personnel to its staff in order to continue giving the same high level of care.

Because of the extraordinarily labor-intensive nature of services to those with handicaps, 159 staff members comprising three shifts were needed to teach and care for 128 students around the clock. One reason for this high ratio is that unlike blind students, students with profound retardation cannot fill "down time" and greater numbers of staff are needed to keep them engaged in productive activities throughout the day.

Some people in the community who had always defined Oak Hill as one of the nation's pre-eminent schools for the blind resisted the trend to include students with severe disabilities. However, never an institution to cater to societal expectations, Oak Hill was determined, in Guldager's words, "to care for the kids no other educators wanted" — just as it always had. It was, after all, the children's needs, and not the school's philosophy, that had changed.

In 1976, Oak Hill staff and students had begun the brave and pioneering foray into "the real world" when the Connecticut Institute for the Blind (CIB), the umbrella organization under whose aegis Oak Hill operates, opened up its first group residence, an eight-room colonial in Windsor called the Pace Home, named for Josephine Pace.

This group home, which was only the first of dozens, signified a shift to a more statewide, community-based emphasis at the institution. By 1986, in just the one decade since the first group home opened, forty others, along with eight vocational day programs, were in full operation. Soon, many other community residences would spring up throughout the state like mountain laurel blossoms, bearing proud testimony to the resilient spirits of those giving — and receiving — the care.

"Each time you develop a house, you must look at the needs of the individuals," says Stan Soby, director of group homes for CIB. "Each home must be planned so that the emotional, as well as the physical, needs of each resident are taken into account."

Soby believes that the intimate scale of CIB's community residences, which average six residents versus fifteen in some nearby states, contributes to the individual and collective success of the home's occupants.

"The dynamics and the intensity of life change directly in proportion to the size," says Soby. "What were challenging behaviors at Mansfield Training School diminish in a group home of six residents, and may disappear altogether in a home of three. We've seen it again and again, so we're trying to develop smaller locations so the relationships can grow more fully with the greater space for each person."

In 1986, Oak Hill took another radical step. Although at an all-time high of 231 students, the school closed enrollment to its campus program and began, in effect, to deinstitutionalize itself. Oak Hill moved Connecticut students into community based homes and into classroom and work settings in the community. And the school worked with out-of-state school districts to move students back into their home states to be closer to their families and the services they would need as adults.

The results of such a move could have been problematic. Unlike their blind predecessors, after graduation, these Oak Hill students had only one option open to them: to be sent home to families ill-prepared to meet their needs while their names were placed on waiting lists for services.

School districts paid the costs of group home living until the student reached the age of twenty-one, but funding was uncertain after that.

Seeking to avert a crisis for these students, Oak Hill found a solution by reaching an unprecedented agreement with then-Commissioner of the Department of Mental Retardation Brian Lensink. Under the terms of this compact, CIB agreed to continue to build community group homes for its

CIB/OHS PROGRAM LOCATIONS

(All are in Connecticut)

GROUP HOMES AND SUPPORTED LIVING

Andover
Ansonia
Bloomfield
Bolton
Bozrah
Broad Brook
Burlington
Cheshire
Colchester
Collinsville
Columbia
Coventry
Durham
East Hartland
Enfield
Farmington
Glastonbury
Granby
Hebron
Lebanon

Manchester
Mansfield
New Hartford
Newington
Norwich
Orange
Rocky Hill
Shelton
Simsbury
Southbury
Suffield
Torrington
Vernon
Wallingford
Waterbury
Watertown
West Hartford
Wethersfield
Windsor

DAY SERVICES

Ansonia
Bloomfield
East Hartford
Hartford
Naugatuck
Seymour
Simsbury
Waterbury
Windsor
Woodbridge

EDUCATION

Hartford
New Hartford
Simsbury
Marlborough

older students by using federal Housing and Urban Development (HUD) funds (thus saving the state considerable amounts of money). The Department, for its part, pledged to continue the funding for these Connecticut students after they had turned twenty-one. This insured a home and work in the community for Connecticut's Oak Hill graduates so long as the Legislature appropriates funds for the Department.

"The agreement has meant phenomenal peace of mind to many parents," says Rebecca D. Earl, assistant executive director of Oak Hill. "It allows us to continue what we've started with our students and means they can continue working toward their maximum independence in an environment that is both supportive and challenging."

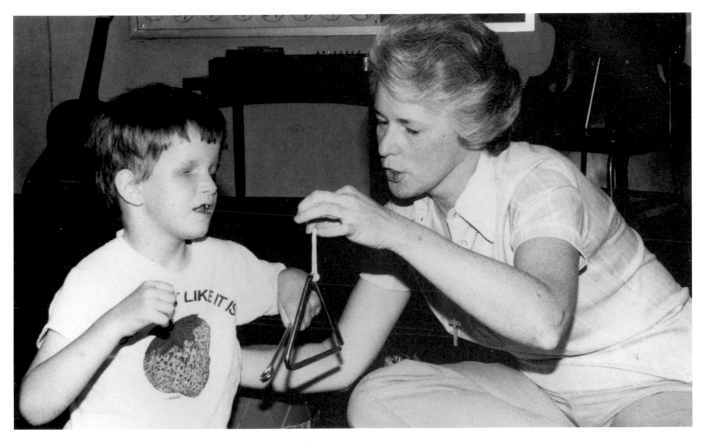

Music therapy often helped students express themselves.

One Hundred Years of Service  & Beyond

1985 – Present

*It proved the truth one must discover for oneself — that perception
is achieved with what Helen Keller called "eyes in the mind."*

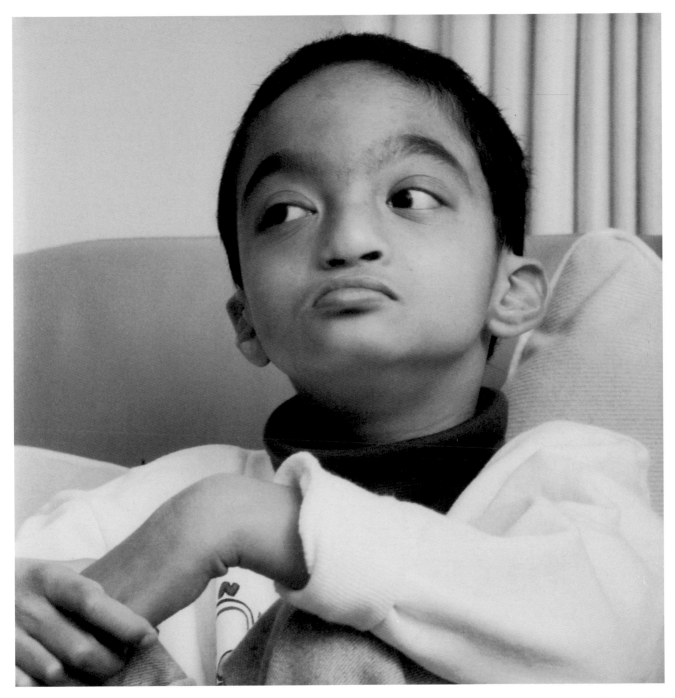

Rhey Alcid.

Adaptive equipment is a boon to student and teacher alike.

A daycare student on the campus today.

On the job in the cafeteria of Aetna Life & Casualty.

Vocational training boosts morale and skills.

"Sympathy, like the atmosphere, surrounds us on every side, but like the atmosphere, is too light to sustain life. To acknowledge that our present work may have faults and imperfections, is only to admit that it has been produced by human agency. But we certainly cannot ask to have them excused or loved in consequence of our peculiar condition..."

This quotation comes from an unnamed author of a book entitled *Achievements of the Blind,* published by Artman & Hall of Rochester N.Y. in 1872. The volume was a favorite of Frank Cleaveland's, and he cited it often when trying to appeal to the public for critical analysis of, rather than mere sympathy for, the blind community's position in life.

The anonymous source of this quote was referring to the condition of blindness, not mental retardation, neurological impairment, or any of the other physical conditions in which Oak Hill, by the dawn of the 1990s, had become so proficient. And yet there is much resonance in these words. Sympathy alone may heal some wounds. But it will never foster independence and self-sufficiency in those capable of it, and it will never provide protection for those whose lives depend on it.

Training people with disabilities and caring, day by day, for those incapable of caring for themselves, surely starts with sympathy, but it moves immediately on to expertise, hard work and financial resources. It is these last three qualities which, when brought to bear in serving children and adults with special needs, create the strength that separates Oak Hill from other well-meaning, sympathetic groups.

In its one hundred years of service, Oak Hill has consistently garnered this strength, both as an institution and as individuals within it. When

Emily Wells Foster decided to make a difference in the lives of Connecticut's blind residents, she learned to speak a new language, studied the medical ramifications of the condition and sought advice on educational methods. In other words, she developed the expertise she would need to meet her enormous challenge. That she put in years of hard work is indisputable and that she and her colleagues struggled mightily to obtain the necessary funds is also documented in the annals of state government and private philanthropy.

In a very real sense, then, Foster set a tone for the institution which lasts today. While the mission has broadened enormously and the methodology has, of necessity, been revolutionized, there is at the core of the institution's work this same triune — expertise, hard work and an ever-expanding need for resources.

Under the leadership of Lars Guldager and the guidance of the Board of Directors, the institution constantly looks for new ways to develop expertise and apply it wherever it is needed in the field — in short, new ways to be helpful.

One way in which Oak Hill is finding new educational territory is in the treatment and care of persons with Prader-Willi Syndrome, a genetic disorder caused by the deletion of part of the fifteenth chromosome. The condition, which affects an estimated one in fifteen thousand babies, manifests itself in extreme behavior and eating disorders.

Prader-Willi robs the person of the ability to control food cravings and often results in obesity and serious psychological problems such as uncontrollable anger and sleep disorders. Other physical anomalies often accompany the condition, including scoliosis, impaired speech, strabismus, infertility, and certain forms of diabetes.

Currently, ten persons with Prader-Willi reside in CIB group homes. Although most of these residents live in homes with residents who do not have the syndrome, one home in Bolton serves only persons with Prader-Willi. June Smith has been the home's manager since it opened in 1987.

"All of the staff and I have known the great joy and satisfaction of seeing fewer and fewer behavior problems in our residents with Prader-Willi," Smith says. "Sometimes it's hard for them to control their actions because they tend to see things in black and white terms, and that often leads to extremes of behavior. But in a small group setting, they learn to compromise and their social skills improve markedly. It's a wonderful thing to see, because these people are really enjoyable to be with. They can be stubborn, but they have many great qualities, too, such as humor and generosity."

Smith says that although mental retardation is almost always a part of the Prader-Willi condition, its form is usually mild. She adds that as diagnoses are made earlier than in the recent past, so too can intervention and training begin earlier. Consequently, very young people with the condition are making strides their older Prader-Willi peers have not made.

"Our residents show great variety in their personalities and their skills — they can read, write, use calculators and get a great deal out of a field trip. Working with them is as rewarding as it is challenging."

She cites the story of Jeff, a twenty-five-year-old resident of the home in Bolton. He is talkative, friendly, well-travelled and well-dressed. He loves the theater, goes to church regularly and recently participated in a local "Walk Against Hunger." And yet, Jeff is set apart from much of society because of his condition.

"When Jeff came to us, he was about seventy pounds overweight and unhappy," says Smith. "Today, he is at his goal weight, is very social, a lot of fun, and, unfortunately for me sometimes, very clever! He's always one up on us, and we have to be thinking in ten different directions at once."

One of the hallmarks of Prader-Willi Syndrome is that it is very difficult for people with the condition to understand the connection between actions and consequences. For this reason, Cedric Newman, Jeff's job coach at his mail clerk position, is pleased with Jeff's progress. Even in situations that are potentially stressful for a person with Prader-Willi, such as being in a lunch room, Jeff has learned to control his impulses. "Jeff has never been a challenge in terms of his job skill level," Newman says, "and it's becoming easier to help him stay on track with his personal progress."

While some may criticize the institution for tackling a condition so very far afield from the school's original intent, Guldager and his staff believe it's a natural outgrowth of the early compassionate care given to society's outcasts.

There is, undeniably, a radical difference between the early students, whose only disability was blindness, and today's students, many of whom cannot even comprehend the simplest achievements of the school's earlier graduates. And yet, they have in common the fact that they all, in their own time, were set apart from the rest of society by a physical condition over which they had no control. Here is where Oak Hill's vision for children and adults with disabilities sees through society's darkness. And more than once, it was a vision which threw light there.

Mary Cheney, the first woman to serve as Chair of the Board's Executive Committee, is a longtime director, supporter and member of the Ladies Visiting Committee. She was instrumental in proving to sighted society that there are many ways of "seeing." Cheney, who enjoys a lifelong interest in art, was an active member of the Docent Council of the Wadsworth Atheneum. She has also long been an ardent supporter of Oak Hill students.

In 1972, she combined these two passions when she developed, on behalf of the Ladies Visiting Committee, a feasibility study for a new "touch gallery" in the Atheneum. The Lions Gallery of the Senses, which operated for decades as one of the most exciting art venues the city had ever known, opened up worlds of art to the blind and disabled, and showed visually oriented art lovers that there are many, often deeper, ways to experience beauty.

"My longtime interest in perception and my interest in work with the multiply disabled students of Oak Hill fused together with a totally new significance during the development of the gallery," Cheney says. "It was very gratifying, because the disabled visitor's enthusiastic response to the exhibits helped to convince the general public of the validity of the gallery concept for the exploration of perception. It proved the truth one must discover for oneself — that perception is achieved with what Helen Keller called *eyes in the mind.* I believe beauty is not in the eye of the beholder, but in the brain, which is blind."

Perhaps it is this "blindness" to societal norms and expectations that has guided Oak Hill educators all along. Certainly they did not heed skeptical warnings when, in the 1970s, the institution began to open small group homes where those with multiple disabilities could live peaceful, stimulating lives.

"Although the concept of a small group home, rather than a large institution, nursing home or moderate sized facility may still seem radical to some people, it's actually based on a very traditional premise — the nuclear family," says Guldager. "We believe the best place for a child is with his parents, whenever possible, but that is frequently not the case for many of our students. So in the homes, we use a nuclear family model and the home manager becomes, in many cases, like a mother or father. We try to be as creative as we can in making an abnormal situation feel normal. That's where the staff become advocates for our clients. If a manager says 'Mary or Joe — do you want to go shopping for jeans?' it may restrict the rest of the group for a while, but that's the way real families work. The residents learn that each of them is important in his or her own way and each deserves the right to happiness and attention. Some so-called 'experts' may argue with the practicality of this kind of highly individualized care, but that's what works and so that's what we do."

Terry Roberts, regional director for the Department of Mental Retardation, is one of many in the social service field who rely on Oak Hill's expertise. Under Roberts' direction, 301 clients have been placed in CIB-run community residences. In addition, the Department has authorized 123 clients to participate in CIB day programs. The Department began funding CIB group homes in 1984, and it was a decision of which Roberts is proud.

"Time and again, I've seen the positive results of each placement," Roberts says without hesitation. "If someone comes to us needing a placement for a family member, and when placements were needed for the residents of the old Mansfield Training School, we turn to Oak Hill. From the beginning, Oak

Hill has been a partner in trying to develop opportunities for homelike settings through which our clients can really be a part of a community. The staff is well-trained and caring, and they're not hesitant about taking risks that let the client grow more independent. As a group charged with quality assurance, Oak Hill is very responsive. And as an advocacy-oriented institution, they've almost always won the day."

Roberts also cites Oak Hill's technological expertise as a crucial element in the institution's record of success.

"They continue to grow and change," she explains. "The staff know how to apply technological advances in computers and switches, for example, to the everyday lives of the people in their care. It's this creativity that gives people a better life. I think what impresses me most, though, is how

They continue to grow and change…The staff know how to apply technological advances in computers and switches, for example, to the everyday lives of the people in their care. It's this creativity that gives people a better life. I think what impresses me most, though, is how the staff tailor the treatment and methodology to the individual client.

the staff tailor the treatment and methodology to the individual client. Oak Hill has a wide spectrum of clients with vastly differing needs and abilities. They have terrific homes for the geriatric disabled, for example, which integrate recreational day programs into the clients' living arrangement. Oak Hill is a leader in that area. But that's typical — they're in the forefront of everything."

Today, the Connecticut Institute for the Blind operates sixty group homes in thirty-nine communities, serving more than 350 adults and students. In addition to these homes and to the Oak Hill School itself, CIB runs four supported living arrangements through which the organization helps clients who are retarded to live independently, ten day vocational programs, a daycare center, a training department, and an adaptive equipment shop.

The institution's adaptive equipment department is a national leader in the innovative reconstruction and altering of equipment needed by children with profound disabilities. Unable to perform simple tasks most of us take for granted, such as buttoning a shirt or sitting upright, many of Oak Hill's students need physical support to back up the emotional support they receive.

In the adaptive equipment shop, located on the Holcomb Street campus, specialist Gary Alff and his small staff make big strides in helping students perform the many individual tasks that lengthen into a twenty-four-hour day.

Frustrated by the preponderance of mass-produced equipment ill-suited to the unique needs of Oak Hill's children, the staff began to tinker with wheelchairs, braces and other things that special needs pupils require. Much as a classic auto collector searches for an obscure part or the exact shade of 1967 cherry red, Alff and his crew hunt up the perfect bolt to hold a transfer board at just the right angle for a child with a muscular deformation. Or, they'll figure out

Recreational activities in the community are an important part of the Oak Hill program. Here, adaptive equipment makes bowling at a public lane possible.

how to adapt a wheelchair's head-rest for a particular child who may have trouble turning to the left, but not the right. A different child, who can turn his head to the right and *not* the left, needs a different chair. At Oak Hill, he has one made for him.

In 1990, the Connecticut Institute for the Blind began to market these specially designed adaptive products to other service providers, such as the Department of Mental Retardation, medical supply houses and nursing homes. But it is with Oak Hill's own clients that one can most easily see the remarkable changes the adaptive equipment can make in a young person's life. One such person is Rhey Alcid.

Rhey is a fourteen-year-old resident of CIB's Collins House in Collinsville. There are many ways to describe Rhey. Medically, he is a child with Wolf-Hirschhorn Disease, a syndrome in which a part of chromosome number four is missing and in which the patient bears several congenital anomalies and experiences severely delayed mental and physical development.

Because of the slow growth, progress is measured in small increments and each accomplishment is a major triumph. For example, when Rhey finally took his first independent steps, at age thirteen, staff in other community residences and across the Oak Hill campus rejoiced.

Physically, Rhey must be described as wraithlike, with large, dark eyes, and fingers long and slender as reeds. At most, he looks seven years old.

But to describe Rhey by these traits alone is to miss his most obvious characteristics. He is an energetic cyclist, climbing aboard his bike — hand-tailored with special pedals at the Holcomb Street shop — and wheeling enthusiastically around the patio of his group home. He is an indefatigable tour-guide, grabbing the nearest hand and leading a visitor from one resident's bedroom to another, pausing just long enough for the newcomer to take in the toys, stuffed animals and decorations that adorn each room. He is an avid basketball fan, rarely missing a UConn Huskies game on television. And finally, despite the fact that he cannot speak, he is a flirt, easily moving among staff and guests, flashing an irresistible smile.

"Everyone loves Rhey," says Beth Wiblyi, manager of the group home in Collinsville. "He's so agreeable and loving and he's responsive, too. He enjoys just about everything we do here. Rhey is one reason this place really feels like family."

Along with his four house-mates, Rhey has shown his local community that people with physical and intellectual disabilities can add immeasurably to the lives of the rest of us. Rhey and his house-mates, who range in age from fourteen to twenty-one, were the last of

Teacher and student share a quiet, comforting moment on the Holcomb Street campus.

Oak Hill's Connecticut students to leave the Holcomb Street campus for life in a community residence. They attend an education program at the Ann Antolini School in New Hartford, where several fifth and sixth graders vie for the right to read to the Oak Hill students and teach them computer skills.

It's often hard to tell who feels better about the exchange — the public school students, many of whom are exposed for the first time to children with physical and mental disabilities — or the Oak Hill students, who seem to relish the chance to interact daily with their new friends.

Oak Hill, to foster such community involvement and community experience for its students, leases space for its classrooms from public schools wherever it is feasible. The results are often surprising.

For example, when Lis Phillips, an Oak Hill teacher at the Henry James Middle School of Simsbury, volunteered to teach sign language to the regular students and staff so they could communicate better with the Oak Hill students, she was overwhelmed with requests.

To the untutored eye, it seems like a miracle, but to Anna Eddy, director of education at Oak Hill, "it's what happens naturally when people get to know our kids."

For older Oak Hill clients, education includes vocational training. Through the intensive vocational training at Holcomb Street and in the ten adult day programs across the state, people with

LIFE WITH PETER

Robert and Barbara Cloonan of West Hartford, Connecticut, are the parents of twenty-three-year-old Peter Cloonan, who is severely disabled. Peter has been at Oak Hill since 1976. He is a resident of CIB's Hickory Hill home in East Granby. The following is their combined testimonial about their life with Peter and their relationship with Oak Hill.

Peter was two months old when Bob was transferred from Albany to Tulsa by Aetna. It was during his first checkup in this new location that doctors first gave us the news that Peter was blind. It would not be until two years later that we would discover he was also deaf. As the result of another transfer, we moved to Hartford when Peter was six. By then, it was becoming more clear that Peter's disabilities were extensive and his progress would be measured in very small steps.

When we first enrolled Peter at Oak Hill, the school offered only a day program — five days a week and no summers or weekends. However, when he was eight, they began the residential program. Peter was also at Oak Hill when they expanded from a school for deaf/blind children to a school and residential facility for multihandicapped kids and adults.

Oak Hill had an excellent national reputation as a school for the blind, but we must admit that we were nervous when we looked at the challenge Peter presented.

Fortunately, we soon learned that Oak Hill's reputation was growing, primarily because the new superintendent, Lars Guldager, brought many great changes and new ideas with him. It was an expansion in philosophy aimed particularly at children like Peter.

Two of Oak Hill's strong points are its teaching staff and home care workers. They have always been a real asset. When the school changed from day to residential, the learning and care expanded greatly, because now there were two separate staffs. There was not only much more going on, but there was also the ability to incorporate daily living skills and vocational training. Each group of teachers had new energy and a fresh approach. This is when we realized that Oak Hill was able to provide a much more complete and consistent program for Peter than we could ever offer him at home. The staff was able to give much more "quality time." We've found, too, that all the teachers are accepting and dedicated. In this kind of work, if you're not committed to what you're doing, you don't last very long.

We've always felt quite comfortable with the people who've taken care of him. They're attentive, caring, and, most importantly, they treat each person with dignity and respect. This is probably the number one hope that parents have and we feel fortunate that Oak Hill encourages this. In addition to a sense that Oak Hill is his home, this special care and companionship are probably a big part of the reason why his behavior has improved so over the years. We don't see any more of the tantrums and the kind of frustration that used to be commonplace. Although Peter still has no speech and has extremely limited sign-language capabilities, he is able to communicate his basic needs and is comfortable in familiar surroundings. He enjoys his visits home (we think it's the good cooking and loose rules that allow him to get away with a bit more!) but he always seems happy to jump in the van and go back to Hickory Hill.

His home and support staff as well as the O.P.S. (Overall Plan of Service) team work closely with us to develop a plan for his care. Oak Hill is very involved in the decisions, but we always feel that, as Peter's parents, the ultimate decisions — especially on medical matters — should be ours. Oak Hill is very supportive and understanding of this.

One of the things that makes such a difference to us, as the parents of a disabled young man, is to know that our son is becoming part of a community. While we believe that we still have a long way to

go before true acceptance as neighbors is achieved, at Oak Hill, the residents are given a chance to live as close to "normal" as the rest of us do. The general public may not see the benefits of taking severely disabled young people to the movies or on a shopping trip, but it's invaluable to Peter, and to us.

And at his group home, he's really in a family setting. His friends know their own rooms, and they know and trust the people with whom they share their lives. It takes a while for outsiders to appreciate, but these young people are wonderful and unique. If we had one wish for young people like our son, it would be that society would realize these people have feelings, emotions and personalities just as we do. They cannot express themselves in the same way, but, still, if one has the time and patience to hold a hand or give a hug, they can experience the love these young people offer. When people take the time to get to know them, and to open their minds and hearts, they're always a little better for it; that's the effect these "kids" have.

Recently, as we put Peter on the van to go back to Hickory Hill, Christie, who is one of his housemates, reached over and buckled Peter's seat belt. You see, each of them, no matter how disabled, has something to offer this world.

severe retardation learn productive skills such as assembling packages, sorting materials, applying labels and preparing mailings for corporations and agencies such as Heublein, Latex Foam Company of Ansonia, the Connecticut Public Expenditures Council, Child and Family Services and CIB's own internal needs.

With training and supervision, they learn to clean apartment buildings, deliver newspapers and other tasks which clearly contribute to society.

Al Heinzmann, director of adult day programs, believes that through such programs "people with disabilities come to know they are contributors to society, not just recipients of society's charity. They feel productive, which is important for all of us to feel."

Heinzmann adds that the very presence of Oak Hill clients in the mainstream has educated society as a whole.

"Even ten years ago, people with severe disabilities wouldn't have had the opportunities to

RECENT U.S. MILESTONES
FOR PEOPLE WITH DISABILITIES

1967   Legislative enactment of Section 10-76 of the Connecticut General Statutes ensuring special education services to Connecticut school children

1972   Landmark consent decree in the case of Pennsylvania Association for Retarded Citizens v. Commonwealth of Pennsylvania upheld the rights of children with mental retardation to receive a free, appropriate education

1973   Passage of the federal Rehabilitation Act prohibiting discrimination on the basis of handicap

1976   Passage of the federal Education of all Handicapped Children Act (Public Law 94-142) guaranteeing a free, appropriate public education for all school children to age 21 in the least restrictive environment

1988   Consent decree in the case of the Connecticut Association for Retarded Citizens v. Gareth Throne, which ultimately resulted in the closing of the Mansfield Training School in 1993

1990   Public Law 94-142 amended, now called Individuals with Disabilities Act (IDEA)

1991   Passage of the Americans with Disabilities Act, which prohibits discrimination against people with disabilities in all sectors of society and all aspects of life

interact with society the way our clients do," he says. "It's a great thing to see the relationships that develop. Our job coaches have taught some of the condo and apartment residents a little sign language and they're fond of giving our clients the 'Hi' sign when they come to vacuum. It's little things like this that teach the rest of society what we at Oak Hill have known for a long time: people with disabilities should not be placed in institutions. Now, through programs like ours, I feel the rest of society is catching on."

Although their skill levels are dramatically lower than those of their blind forebears at Oak Hill, today's students experience a similar satisfaction at having accomplished more than is expected of them by a public unaware of their potential.

"My observation is that they really feel good about completing something and doing it right," says Anna Eddy. "Because this is contract work, they are paid for their time and skills, according to their level, and a paycheck for them is the same as for any of us — it's highly motivating. More importantly, though, they feel good about being praised for their accomplishments."

And so it becomes a part of the main "domains" of a student's education at Oak Hill through which he or she learns four kinds of skills: vocational, domestic, community and recreational.

It may seem a far cry from the skills Emily Foster taught. And yet, despite all the radical changes the institution has willingly brought upon itself over its one hundred years, it has forgotten neither its roots, nor the early struggles of its blind students who yearned for acceptance and independence.

This understanding still guides Oak Hill today. For example, Oak Hill is once again looking ahead, trying to find ways to take the independence of the group home setting even farther. Recognizing that some residents can handle more independence than a group home affords, Oak Hill is working with the Department of Mental Retardation to create supported living arrange-ments though which clients who do not necessarily require someone to live with them still get the help they need in areas such as grocery shopping, menu planning and banking.

Other clients wish simply to communicate. In 1993, on the one hundredth anniversary of its founding, the school opened the Ella Victoria Anderson Resource Room. In this special room, named for a sighted donor who eventually became blind, is a machine that "reads" out loud anything in print. What's more, the machine can print out this material in Braille. Eventually, all who use the machine, in particular the school's graduates, will be able simply to speak into the mouthpiece and have their words printed out in Braille.

In some perfect parallel, this machine harks back to the school's early teaching devices — the grooved boards and rudimentary Braillers — because it breaks old rules and creates new possibilities for people with special needs.

That is why when people like Josephine Pace, Robert and Barbara Cloonan, Lars Guldager, Craig Cody and others at Oak Hill look at the future, they see both accomplishment and change. Or, in Guldager's words, "we see what needs to be done, and then we do more. Because when it comes to human achievement, sight is far less important than vision."

If ever this vision were in doubt, one need only look into the eyes of a child like Rhey Alcid, which focus on less than our eyes, but which see, in some special way, far more.

The fingertips "see" all in reading Braille.

A DAY IN THE LIFE OF A GROUP HOME

Residents of the Vernon group home gather for a "family photo."

It's four o'clock on a Wednesday afternoon. Classes are done for the day, Oprah is over, the house is picked up and it's too early to start dinner. So what do six "girls" do for fun? Throw a cucumber facial party, of course.

Looking around the living room of the group home she manages in Vernon, Kim Lange sees Diane, J.J., Robin, Donna, Pauline and Annie flopping in couches, armchairs and one wheelchair, their faces smeared in sea green facial mud and their eyes covered with cucumber slices. Two of the young women are taking the treatment very seriously; the others are hooting with delight and trying to keep the cukes from sliding down their cheeks.

"It's not usually this wild," Lange remarks, and then adds, "Well, yeah, I guess it often is..."

The twin cockatiels Eliot and E.T. squawk from on top of the cage where they perch imperiously. A wreath of dried purple heather brightens a bedroom wall. Somebody wrapped in a terrycloth robe pads out of the bathroom after a shower. Somebody else works diligently at a computer ter-

minal. More than one bed sports a reclining teddy bear. And in the kitchen, there's a great debate raging: the relative merits of peanut butter versus chocolate chip cookies.

With its air of camaraderie, trust and innocent hi-jinx, the Vernon home could almost be a college dorm.

"All of our girls are hearing impaired and visually impaired and I guess you'd have to say that, technically, they function in the moderate range of retardation," says Lange. "But in truth, none of us staff members think of them that way. To us they're family — we love them, get a little frustrated with them sometimes and have high expectations of them, just as you would your own sisters."

Lange easily points out the changes each of the women has shown since moving into the home.

"J.J. grew up at the Mansfield Training School. Jo Pace saw her fending off the other patients and made moves to get her out of there. When she came to us she was very shy and retiring — she hung back a lot." As if on cue, J.J. runs into the room with her favorite picture of her idol, Oprah Winfrey, in which the talk show host stands beside a beaming J.J. on the studio lot.

"Diane also was very insecure when she came to us," Lange goes on. "Recently, though, she was named 'Employee of the Year' at BESB, where she holds a job as a contract worker (putting tie cords into the waistbands of sweat pants for the U.S. military). The staff here really worked on building Diane's self-esteem, by training her at the computer and helping her learn to cook. Now, she does all kinds of things for herself, including administering her own medications. She never used to ask for anything. Now, she even talks back to us, which is actually a wonderful thing — it's

Donna pulls a practical joke on Kim Lange, group home manager.

a sign of an intact ego, not a fragile one."

For each of the residents, the story is just as encouraging. Lange credits a combination of the clients' own indomitable spirits and the staff's dedication. Most of the eight staff members have been with the Vernon home since it opened in 1986.

As a farewell gesture to the day's visitors, Donna, who looks remarkably like the actress Genevieve Bujold, begins to untie her right sneaker. Slowly, she removes the shoe, then the sock, as Lange asks her several times what she's doing.

"Does your foot hurt? Do you have a sliver? Are you showing us some new socks?" Lange wants to know.

Finally, sensing the perplexity among staff and visitors, Donna holds up her sneaker triumphantly and grins.

Diane works at the computer in her Vernon group home.

All the women in the room — staff and residents alike — break into laughter: Donna was merely having a rather elaborate joke at our expense.

Staffer Suzanne Plover, wiping the facial mud off Diane, explains that these sorts of loving pranks are commonplace occurrences. "That's why it feels like family," she says simply and adds, "I really love the clients, as well as the staff. When one girl is ill, or has a doctor's appointment, all the others will hover around her to make sure she's okay. That kind of compassion is very moving and makes all the difference in a job like mine. Truthfully, I can't imagine another home I'd like better."